Wakefield

INVISIBLE MENDING

At the age of seventeen, Mike Ladd began reading his poetry at Adelaide's renowned Friendly Street and his poems started appearing in local and national publications. His first book *The Crack in the Crib* was published in 1984 followed by eight collections of poetry and prose.

Mike was the editor of ABC Radio National's highly respected *Poetica*, which ran for eighteen years. He currently works for Radio National's features and documentary unit, and he and his partner Cathy Brooks have been running projects that put poems on street signs as public art. Mike is a poetry mentor, judge, and also a reviewer for the *Sydney Morning Herald*. Over the past two decades he has given poetry workshops and masterclasses in every state and territory of Australia.

Mike Ladd lives in Adelaide.

By the same author

The Crack in the Crib, Friendly Street Poets, 1984

Picture's Edge, Friendly Street Poets in association
with Wakefield Press, 1994

Close to Home, Five Islands Press, 2000

Rooms and Sequences, Salt Publishing, 2003

Shacklife, Picaro Press, 2006

Transit, Five Islands Press, 2007

*Karrawirra Parri – Walking the Torrens from Source
to Sea,* Wakefield Press, 2012

Adelaide, Garron Publishing, 2014

Invisible Mending

MIKE LADD

Photographs by Cathy Brooks

Wakefield
Press

Wakefield Press
16 Rose Street
Mile End
South Australia 5031
www.wakefieldpress.com.au

First published 2016
Reprinted 2018

Copyright © Mike Ladd, 2016

All rights reserved. This book is copyright. Apart from any fair dealing for the
purposes of private study, research, criticism or review, as permitted under
the Copyright Act, no part may be reproduced without written permission.
Enquiries should be addressed to the publisher.

Cover designed by Liz Nicholson, designBITE
Edited by Julia Beaven, Wakefield Press
Text designed and typeset by Wakefield Press

National Library of Australia Cataloguing-in-Publication entry

Creator: Ladd, Mike, 1959–   , author.
Title: Invisible mending // Mike Ladd; photographs by Cathy Brooks.
ISBN: 978 1 74305 407 9 (paperback).
Subjects: Ladd, Mike, 1959– .
               Australian poetry – 21st century.
               Short stories, Australian – 21st century.
               Australian essays – 21st century.
Other Creators/Contributors: Brooks, Cathy, photographer.
Dewey Number: A821.3

CORIOLE
McLAREN VALE

Contents

Foreword

In this accelerated mix of poetry and prose Mike Ladd is all the while needling complacency. 'Once I thought you were too small, /but after all these years we fit each other', he writes of his home town, Adelaide, the habitat charms of which he celebrates 'as the place is talked up and gets its festival clothes on'. But what's to become of us in such a cushy bourgeois nest? Ladd delivers flinty visionary poems as he drives north to *The Golden Highway, Thinking of Global Warming.* He passes sheep stations with their 'concentration camp' hair; he gets to the 'battered, holy ground' of dirt roads where 'termite statues … grow into roadside gods: Buddhas Shivas Madonnas Lingams Christs Tjurungas'. He draws the landscapes politically/spiritually as they double bind the late middle-aged suburban man: 'What sustains me, what makes me alone … There's no easy way out of here.'

In fact, there's no easy way anywhere, really. Not when he is immersed in a Malaysian village writing deceptively sedate pantuns; not when the imagination, his and ours, must endure the *Museum of Memory, Santiago de Chile*; least of all when he contemplates activists who self-immolate – the *Gasoline Flowers* of recent history.

Such poems are made to hurt and they do, while the prose of *Invisible Mending* – closely observed, charged with uncertainties and dreamscapes – is also intent on our awakening. It travels towards the Other – newly arrived Sudanese boys, petty criminals in South-East Asia, even a son who turns out to be Other when he comes back from Colombia full of silent provocation. Meanwhile Mike Ladd is engaged in the silent mending of grief for his late father, which gives his whole trajectory here its burnished realism.

Barry Hill

A Neighbour's Photo

They appear suddenly in the dogbox flats behind us. Arwan and Niall, tall and slim and Sudan black. A generation ago they would have become 'Alan and Neil,' but now at least they can keep their names intact. Arwan is about thirteen. He meets our son on the school oval one evening. He says his older brother Niall is angry with him and he doesn't want to go back to the flat. Their mother is in a refugee camp in Kenya and their father is still in Sudan – doing what, we never find out. Niall, at eighteen, is Arwan's guardian. They walked thirty days from Sudan into Kenya and now here they are, stark against our horizon of cream-brick flats, trying to learn a new language, trying to understand how this place works.

This place where dogs are fed fresh chicken breasts, and swimming pools are fenced-off for the exclusive use of just two people. This place where the religious days are as mixed as the styles of food and it's all 'go easy, cruise along, don't take too much interest', but thon suddenly a minor traffic incident makes strangers explode into punch-throwing violence. These dead-quiet streets interrupted by hotted-up cars driven by men yelling out something savage as they go past. This place where the magpies sing and the eucalypts form silhouettes against the orange west and their bark clatters and falls to reveal new phosphorous-green and

1

mars-violet skins. In this strange world at evening, Arwan waits out on the oval.

Arwan stutters badly – he's in trouble with his brother because he went out all day without telling Niall where he was. Niall cuffed him about the head when he came home, so he ran out and has been wandering the suburb. Now that it's dark he's worried Niall will be even angrier. He shows us a bruise above his elbow, 'My ... brother ... he ... hit ... me.' His stutter is a series of gasps before each word, a gulping for air. We're not sure how much English he understands. When our son brings him into the house he doesn't react when we ask if he wants a lemon drink. He stands there observing. I am cooking dinner and he finds this funny, a man in the kitchen chopping vegetables, as odd as a horse in a tree.

We feed him. He's hungry though we can tell he doesn't like the chilli we use in the stir-fry. 'H ... h ... h ... hot,' he says, fanning his tongue. After dinner we go with him to the flat to tell Niall that Arwan has been with us. The front door opens straight into the lounge off a treeless pen of cement enclosed by a high metal fence. Inside there is almost nothing. Two plastic chairs. No television. A couple of beds in the next room. Niall's English is much better – and he speaks another three languages, Swahili, Arabic and Dinka. He explains how hard it is to discipline Arwan. Niall must be the father now, but he's only a teenager himself, and the boy doesn't show him enough respect.

Arwan appears next evening in the middle of our

lounge while we are watching a DVD. One of us turns around and he is simply there, standing quietly in the dark. We explain about knocking on doors and being invited in. Now he is at our front door almost every night. He would like a drink of water. Can he use the telephone? He needs a lift to his married sister's house. He would like to live with his sister but since he has reached puberty, their tradition prevents it. He wants to play with our son. Arwan likes basketball but dislikes the egg shape of Australian Rules footballs. Later, he appears with a half-wrecked pushbike donated by the local church. It has no brakes and its tyres are worn through. The front tyre is flat. I fix the brakes and repair the punctured tube, but tell him it will keep happening with such threadbare tyres. He comes two, three, four times to have punctures repaired. I should really buy him new tyres, but never get around to it. In the end, when our son gets a new bike for his birthday, Arwan inherits the old one.

Arwan's English improves, but his stammer does not. We often wonder what it's like for him in a foreign schoolyard with a stutter like that. He says Niall has 'girlfriends' at the flat and he has to go out. He picks the grapes from our vine without asking. He comes over so often our son says he's sick of him – he's too annoying.

One afternoon Arwan gives us a badly torn black-and-white photograph. The bottom left-hand corner is missing, and the whole picture is crushed and dog-eared. He asks if we could fix it for him. The image shows a young Sudanese woman in a Western tailored dress and an older Sudanese man in a Western suit. They stare seriously, unsmiling and slightly off-centre, at the camera. The stamp at the back of the image says 'Modern Photographers Khartoum'. We imagine the heat and the dusty light outside the studio walls – how sweat patches are hidden in the Western clothes by arms held formally at their sides. Arwan's mother and father in this family portrait are as impersonal as a mugshot. Never the less, this is Arwan's only picture of his mother and as it turns out, the only sight he will have of her for the next several years. We do not understand the delay in his mother's arrival from the Kenyan refugee camp – that is, if she is really there – and we see it causes him distress, so we stop asking him about it. He tells us the man in the photograph is not his father, but his uncle. Another aspect we don't really understand.

Arwan and his brother move out of the dogbox flats. Everything they own fits in one carload. Niall has a factory job and wants to be closer to it. Arwan continues to visit, turning up unannounced, having walked kilometres across the western suburbs. He never phones first. Sometimes our son is not home, and after a glass of water, Arwan walks away again. We had forgotten the photo. My wife pulls it out of a drawer and carefully repairs it with sticky tape and puts it into a spare frame. It waits on a side cupboard for Arwan to collect next time he walks here. Two strangers stare down our hallway, watching the front door.

Adelaide

You old quincunx.
Colonel Light playing tic tac toe
on the Kaurna's pages,
that little brownsnake of a river
winding through its parklands frame.

Over your eastern stairs the sun appears,
filtering through skylights,
the footfall echo of your arcades,
to end with a long bath in the west –
your curve of beaches
which are summer's collective.

Clever, pretty, but lacking confidence,
exposed here on your plain.
We always have to talk you up,
get your festival clothes on.

I like you best in November
when you spill buckets of jacaranda,
April too, when the slow light cools
into shouts in the stadia.
Even now, after a week of 40 degrees –
it's raining at last,
upstairs at the Exeter I can hear
chuckles in the gutters
and applause from the rooftops.

Beyond the brown haze of your suburbs
we smell desert,
so we love to see the water run.

Adelaide – *heimat* of sandstone terraces,
gargoyles, lacunae, suffocations.
Once I thought you were too small,
but after all these years we fit each other:
here in front of Bonython Hall,
my first memory – a pantomime giant
came down through the floodlit trees
chasing Jack and his golden harp.

Place is voice as much as view:
'Legs like Payneham Road'.
'A pash at Windy Point' –
It's better up there than Los Angeles,
that hot glitter, all the way to the Gulf.

Meeting the Ghost of Don Dunstan
on Norwood Parade

He slipped out of the median-strip trees,
carrying a humble bread roll
on a white china plate –
'Here,' he said, 'a gift from the Shades.
You're still dining out at my table.'

Heads turned at the sidewalk cafés,
all the fine-looking women of Norwood
sensing a presence, but still un-fazed.
'You've all gone back to sleep!' Don said,
'I wanted a renaissance, not a dormitory with malls.

I liked Pliny, Parsee eggs, and young men –
and I made a few mistakes.
No one's perfect.
It's necessary to break open some tombs
if you intend to raise a dead state.'

Then parrots shrieked past
flying over the red galvo roof of the grandstand.
Still holding his serving tongs, the ghost began to fade –
disappearing into the listless night
of shop signs and car lights blinking along The Parade.

Learn to Speak the Language

I was on the bus to town.
On the seat in front of me
two women were chatting in Punjabi,
and the guy sitting next to me says:
'If you come to this country
you should learn to speak the language.'

'Yeah. You're right,' I said.
'So how's your Kaurna?
And how good are ya
at Pitjantjatjarra?
Fancy a chat in Ngarkat?

And you know, it's a pity we don't hear
more Peramangk at the bank,
more Tiwi on the TV,
more Wik at the picnic
and Arrente on the verandah.

And, if you expect to live here,
you really oughta
know some Yorta-Yorta,
get your tongue
around Bundjalung,
grasp the meaning in Mirning
and know the score
in Eora.

Kamilaroi and Wiradjuri,
Luritja and Walpiri,
understand their poetry.

You're right, if you come to this country,
You should learn to speak the language.'

Ken

I hear Ken more often than I see him; the crackle and clatter as he flattens aluminium cans and throws them into a wool-bale cover, the clinking as he sorts empty stubbies and longnecks, sometimes late at night. All day he works Prospect Road, between our suburb and the city, checking the garbage bins with a probe. Slowly, the potato-sack he slings over one shoulder grows lumpy with success. Ken used to have a stick from a gum tree to poke through the rubbish, but now he carries an old TV aerial. His hand is hidden by his sleeve and the aerial looks like a strange prosthesis.

Ken's beige puff-jacket is tanned a deeper brown by years of bin-dirt. It matches the colour of his face, scored with deep lines. He has long grey hair to his shoulders and twiggy limbs. Each day he wears the same dirty beige trousers, a colour that seems to be a specialty of the St Vincent de Paul Society. But this is only his work uniform, his hunting and gathering clothes. At other times I see him in a neat grey suit, a white V-neck cardigan underneath, polished R.M. Williams boots, his hair combed over with Californian Poppy. I don't know where he goes on these occasions. Ken has never told me. It's not church. He says he's not into all that – not like the other Aboriginal neighbour next to him, handsome, tweed-jacketed Peter, who's teetotal and a born-again Christian.

Ken says he doesn't drink either, but I've seen him on the bench outside the laundromat or under the portico of the empty church that's been for sale for years. He sits with a small group of men who live in the boarding houses north of here. A couple of them wander the street during the day and one sits on the lawn in the Barker Gardens each evening at sunset, rocking back and forth, talking to himself. With this group, Ken shares large plastic bottles of Coke mixed with some kind of cheap, searing booze. His friend Dave is an outsider to the group, but occasionally joins them. Dave pushes a pram with a black-and-white dog tied to it. Inside the pram, under the baby blankets, are longnecks of beer and a transistor radio. Dave gave Ken a galah for Christmas. The bird is called Col-Col and it lives in a cage on the front porch next to the old lounge chair where Ken spends part of each day watching life in the street. Dave painted 'Col-Col' in fancy letters on a sign that hangs inside the cage.

Ken says, 'The cops in Port Augusta threw me in jail when I was visiting up there because I couldn't walk straight – but that was because I'd broken me ankle. I tripped on a cracked footpath. They said, "Nothing wrong with your ankle, Ken, you're drunk." But I wasn't – just kept blacking out. They wouldn't take me to hospital, so I spent the night in a cell, the swelling spreading up me whole leg. The next morning the sergeant came in and said, "What's up, Ken, what are you in here for?" He knew my family. The sergeant went mad at those young cops and drove me to the hospital himself.'

I don't know if it's because of this incident or something else, but Ken still walks with a limp. One cheekbone is depressed too, an old fracture, never quite fixed. 'I used to be a boxer.' He has blue eyes – 'from an Irish grandfather. I've got Afghan blood as well. When I was young I used to drive supermarket trucks into the Northern Territory – took caffeine pills washed down with cola to stay awake'.

Now he's on the pension and he makes extra from his bottle collecting. It keeps him wiry and fit. He must walk about twenty kilometres a day. Ken sits in his battered chair on his front porch, smoking roll-your-own cigarettes. When they drop off or pick up their children, he lets the mothers from the neighbouring Catholic school park in his driveway, because there's never enough parking in the street, and Ken doesn't have a car. He doesn't rent out the space, never asks for anything, but the women give him presents: cakes, jams and fruit.

Somebody brings Ken a dog, a poor stupid Rottweiler, too big for his yard. He gives it no shelter and feeds it haphazardly, so that it begins to lose weight, its backbone showing under the matt-black fur. Sometimes we throw scraps of food over the fence.

When Ken comes home through his screeching side gate, carrying his sack of bottles and cans, the dog jumps up on him, putting its paws on his twiggy shoulders. It makes him stagger backwards and sideways, cursing and hitting at the dog with his hunting aerial.

In winter we see the dog hunched by our fence, trying to stay out of the bitter rain. So we collect some sheets of galvo and ask Ken if we can build the dog a lean-to kennel. Ken accepts without comment. But a week later the dog gets out of its yard and is running loose in the Catholic school. The police catch it. A female cop, her eyes moist with emotion, comes to our door. 'Do you know who owns the dog? They should be locked up for cruelty to animals. Does it belong to the old Koori next door?' We're not sure who owns the dog. 'It's starving. Look, the bones are coming right through the skin.' Yes, it's terrible we agree, giving the dog some food and watching the poor beast choke it down. 'People don't deserve to have a dog if they treat it that way.' She says she's confiscating the animal but she'll probably take it home herself – she loves Rottweilers. When Ken comes home, his yard and the lean-to kennel are empty. A few days later he asks us if we've seen his dog. We say the cops took it, and he leaves it at that.

One morning Peter dies in his front yard. At first no one sees him. Then, one of the Catholic mothers delivering her child to school spots him lying there under his peach tree – a terrible sight, that handsome black man lying so still under the flourishing tree he had planted. An ambulance is called, but it goes away later without turning on its lights or siren. Ken says it must have been quick, a heart attack. Peter must have come out of his front door then crawled under the tree to die.

Then Ken has new neighbours. An Aboriginal woman and her white husband move in. The man owns a fishing boat. Occasionally the new neighbours throw loud parties, drinking and laughing in the backyard late at night and keeping Ken awake. He doesn't threaten them with the police. Instead, early on Sunday mornings when the neighbours are hung-over, Ken plays Buddy Rich tapes loudly on his stereo, and sits on his steps, listening from outside. He also plays what he calls his 'Dreamtime music' – a CD of didgeridoo from up north.

Spring. A big wind blows in, straight off the Southern Ocean, thumping the limbs of our gleditsia tree against the eaves of our house and breaking off a heavy branch of the red flowering gum. It crushes the fence top and lies halfway across Ken's yard. He's expecting me when I knock on his door. The fallen branch is thick and bifurcates to a network of lesser limbs, then a mass of leaves and red flowers. It looks like a great green and red embroidered ball gown lying over Ken's derelict vegetable patch. All I have are pruning shears and a blunt saw, so it takes me most of the afternoon to cut up the branch and carry it back to my woodpile. Ken's playing his Dreamtime music while I'm sawing. When I ask him to show me the CD, he lets me into his house for the first time.

We go in through the back door, past the kitchen with its laminex table, oddments of cups, the strong, sour smell that cooking cheap cuts of meat leaves behind.

The lounge is neat and sparse, but there's grime on the walls by the light switches. On the cover of the CD, men painted for sacred ceremony are dancing in a circle. Above the hearth, on the mantelpiece, there are some papers, a prescription, a photo of his daughter, but none of his wife. I've never seen her and I don't know what happened to her. Stuck in the middle of the wall above the mantelpiece is a photo of a handsome Aboriginal boy on the edge of manhood. He is beaming with health, smiling straight down the barrel of the camera. The photo is passport-sized, held to the wall by a yellow piece of masking tape.

'Who's that?' I ask Ken.

'That was my son. He hung himself when he was eighteen. His mother found him in the garage. Got into drugs. Nothing I could do.'

He is asking me for something with his eyes. I am inadequate to his need, thinking, Why did there have to be this misery above the hearth, in the centre of this man's home?

'I'm sorry,' I say, 'it's such a …' I stop myself, and we stand looking at each other in the middle of the room.

Summer arrives, more suddenly and fiercely this year. I bring a crate full of empty beer bottles over to Ken's house. He is sitting on his front porch as usual, next to Col-Col who is silent in his cage in the growing heat of the morning. Ken says, 'Woke up in hospital the other day. Just sitting here minding me own business. Must have had a blackout. I used to be a boxer—' (he reminds me again) '—so I get 'em now and then. Someone called an ambulance. Now I've got a five-hundred-dollar bill to pay.' This is the last conversation I will have with Ken. A week later the heatwave arrives. Thirty-nine, forty, forty-two, forty-five degrees. It feels like the city will keep getting hotter, until it finally, simply, ignites. Birds drop out of the sky and die on the softened bitumen. People glance toward the ring of hills above the city, remembering the flaming horizon and wondering if it will come again.

One morning, a police car and an ambulance are parked outside Ken's airless house. Worse, a few days later, his furniture is piled in the driveway and his bottle collection is thrown into a skip. Why didn't his family check? Why didn't he go to one of the neighbourhood cooling centres? Why didn't we keep a better eye on him? Maybe it was just another blackout, a big one.

At his funeral his girls do all the talking. We discover he supported an extended family of children and stepchildren, working for years as a backhoe driver. One of the Catholic school women said he was the face of the street, and the whole neighbourhood would miss him. Dave is in the back row, silent, shaky.

A couple of days later Dave and a few of the men from the boarding houses have a small wake on Ken's empty front porch. Col Col is gone, but his cage is put out on the footpath. The sign with the bird's name has been flipped over, and painted with the single word 'FREE' – and then, a day later, all that is gone too.

Bedroom Ceiling Fan

White medusa
above our reef,
we watch its life-cycle
a fathom down.

In summer it never sleeps,
moving the night's hot breath
on pale, cruciform bodies,
minds refusing to close.

In winter
it lies still,
a three-petalled flower of ice.

It is the turning reel
of our private cinema,
projecting onto these sheets
the amateur porn
of positions we've tried.

Fever sweats,
loneliness,
laughter.

A boring film
where the characters
read books by bedside lights,
and neither speaks.

Times we lie apart in anger,
far as the edges of the bed allow.
Wasted nights.

Here, your waters break twice:
underground springs
no muscle can stop.

Baby heads grow in the white field,
breathing milk,
howling the slow incision of teeth.

The buddhas become long and bony,
flop down between us
wanting to know what to do with their lives –
as we pretend to know.

My black curly hair
greys and shrinks
to a widow's peak.
Your long chestnut waves
are cropped and dyed.

We are buried in the rustle of weekend papers,
their slightly altered, repeating stories:
the greedy privatise gain and socialise loss,
husbands and wives cheat each other, leaders their states,
the so-very-reasonable sell guns to fanatical haters,
people destroy what exists, believing in what doesn't –
and we live in the hegemony of gloss.

On setting one, it is a whisper,
a rumour, a silk dressing gown undone.

On setting two, sweet breezes start to blow.

On setting three, it knocks a rhythm
like the lovers climaxing below.

On setting four, it is a white beehive,
an inner sea, a shallow roar.

On setting five, it is a cyclone's light-bulb eye.

Slow down now, slow down, slow.

Sclerophyll

Even at this distance I can tell
those clouds are rising too fast to be water –

blues and greys of vaporised hills,
an engine trashing itself.

Veiled and shimmering fire, muslin
of summer extinction –

clamour of the news – all the wailing
of some other's cost.

My beautiful eucalypts,
what treacherous bastards you are

now the fire-farmers' ways are lost.

Reveg

This sheep station has
a concentration-camp haircut;

on the stony hill
replanted cypress
forms
a patchy fuzz.

We are growing

two hundred years
of our madness

out.

Night Drive: The Hume

Cath braked hard to save a fox —
eyes points of sodium in the high-beam.
From the back seat
I was launched out of shadow and flare-crossed sleep,
crushed to the blind-black floor by that heavy lover, Inertia.
The tyres screamed into smoke, squared their circle,
and we bumped from then on, all the way to Sydney.

Around another bend we began to see scattered milk bottles,
a lower starry sky —
then the glass truck on its side,
amber pulses and looming cop faces,
the burnt-out wreck of the other truck, and body shapes in blankets.

That was near Jugiong in the small hours,
the cresty bit that helped earn the Hume its 'Deadly' epithet.
All rebuilt now: dual rivers of red and white.

Travelling the Golden Highway, Thinking of Global Warming

Stringybarks in bloom;
a perfume like honey ice-cream.

Along the Prussian escarpment
two eagles work the updraft.

Cicada noise rises and falls
as if the mountain itself was breathing –

In panic.   Out relax.
In panic.   Out relax.

Manga pylons stride the valley,
millions of volts in their fists –

The car radio is plunged into static,
silver grids of capital/energy shift –

Open cuts. Artificial mesas –
Ulan coal warms the world.

Dirt

700 Ks

Alice to Boulia

on the Plenty Highway ...

the dirt

the same colour
as the rusted cans
&
beer bottle
shards.

The termite statues
begin with circles
grow
into roadside gods:

Buddhas

    Shivas

        Madonnas.

Lingams

    Christs

Tjurungas.

This battered,
holy ground.

In a State Forest by the Murrumbidgee

Some things glance off, some go deep.
Even a small voice
returns from across the river.
Mars reflects
in slow, pump-diminished water.

Orion and his dog
hunt the long, soft night
as I try to sort out
the tangle of drought wood
from the good forest:
what sustains,
what makes me alone.

I thought simplicity
was fairer. Camping here
the crumbling banks and the roots
exposed a question:
maybe simplicity and fairness
are opposites?
The track's obscured by fallen trees.
There's no easy way out of here.

Black Swans Mating

At first she is a lone writer
reaching down into the taupe
of the lake.

Feeling for weed-words,
a ribbon of sentence.

Finding a morsel,
she pushes it under herself,
building a book,
a raft for her species.

That black snake of a neck
tipped with red
is constantly scribbling.

Then he arrives, swan-sails in.

She launches
from her self-created island
to glide and moor beside him.

But first the dance.

Chests thumping the water,
beaks dipping,
necks crossways and up and back.

And yes, there are times
when in symmetry
they form the outline
of a ruffled heart in black.

He fast treads water
and lifts onto her,
wings thrown back and beating.

At the peak
they honk and almost squeal
then straighten their necks to the sky.

And who is to say
they don't feel ecstasy,
satisfied lovers
knowing their lover
satisfied as well?

The Cicada Quartets

The cicada plays a guiro,
a wooden scraper
in the throat
of summer.

The cicadas place
their Geiger counters
among the trees.
This must be a lethal dose.

Trapped, the cicada stutters
against the ceiling.
Once, he filled the whole stadium
with his voice.

Cicadas, all day you built
the wall of heat.
Now the thunder has silenced you,
and the rain, ozone sweet.

Cicada, your dried carapace
like pharaoh's winding sheet.
A hollow, full of the
memory of sound.

The Edge of the Lake

You can see the night nurses coming before they arrive; their reflected torch lights bobbing on the ceiling as they walk towards us. Checking us, they click their dolphin lights on and off, creating brief illuminations of our floating faces. Colin says softly, 'Thanks, Mum,' even though the nurse who's bending over his bed is half his age. He's blind and bewildered and it's not until she speaks that he remembers where he is. Before they turned the lights off, he was the first to talk. There are four of us here in this end of the men's ward and it took us most of the afternoon to begin our conversation.

'I was a commercial fisherman at Wallaroo for thirty years,' says Colin, 'until I lost my sight.' He doesn't elaborate. Sometimes he speaks to himself in a small, worried voice – 'I'm hungry. They don't feed you enough in here. Where's my bottle?' When the nurse comes to shower him, she leads him away by the hand, his pale, saggy arse-cheeks revealed by the split in his gown. He looks like a big, hairless baby, learning to walk. 'You're my eyes now, love,' he reminds her. Coming back from the cubicle he says, 'If you were a bit younger, I'd kiss you.' She snorts, gets him back in bed and leaves. After he frets over the position of his urine bottle, coaching himself where to find it, he lies back and begins ...

'I lost my son. He drowned in England. Lake Windermere. He was on holiday. The four of them went

33

out in a boat and they didn't have the plug in the bottom. By the time they woke up to it, the boat was sinking fast. They swam for it. Three got back and one didn't.' We left a silence. What could we say?

'The water was very cold. That was eight years ago. He was only twenty-five.' I get up to go to the toilet. Coming back past Colin's bed he asks, 'Nurse, can you put my call button where I can find it?' and I place it in his hand.

Tom has hard blue eyes behind thick lenses, and shreds of sandy hair growing at the sides of a bald head. He has a fit, wiry body and a left leg ending in a stump below the knee.

'I won't be here long,' he says. 'Beds are for sleeping or rooting. I gotta get back to work driving the mail truck. I used to operate a lift in the mines up at Broken Hill. Eighteen years underground I was. Now I'm on the mail run out to Menindee every day. Wife's doing it, till I get fitted up with a new leg. I'll be back out there soon.' He reaches for his towel. 'I'm diabetic and I didn't know it. This—' (he rubs the swollen stump) '—this started as a little sore on my foot. I got it wet and the sore started growing. Then the guy from the local hospital sent me home with just an alcohol rub. I blame them. It's a meat house, that hospital. When the girl saw it a week later she said, "You're going to the city." It was gangrene. The young surgeon here was trying to save me foot. He took half of it off, but the old bloke, the grumpy one, you'll see him on the rounds, he's the boss, he just said, "Cut your losses," to the young surgeon. "Take it off." Didn't even look me in the face when he said it. Just, "Cut your losses," to the other bloke. That's it.'

'Is it true you can still feel your missing leg?' I ask.

'Yeah, I can still feel me toes. Like I can wiggle them.'

He swivels himself off the bed and lowers his body onto his wheelchair with strong, competent movements, rolling over to the shower now it's free. We believe him when he says he'll be driving the mail truck again. Later, his eyes lose their hardness when he tells us his wife had a breakdown in the truck last week. A drive belt broke and she lost the steering. You can see he loves her and he's worried about her doing the mail run by herself.

'Anyway, I'll be out of here soon,' he says, hoisting himself back into bed, willing himself, prompting us to agree – which we do.

Kevin is in his thirties, tall, strong, a tattoo of a snarling panther on his right shoulder. He's bald as well, but it's from the chemo. He's not a big talker. 'I'm an electrician from Naracoorte. Have to get some stem cells put back into me tomorrow.' Like Colin and Tom, he defines himself with a place and a job. It doesn't sound the same from a city boy having his varicose veins removed. I don't tell them I make radio programs for a living, until they ask. We settle back to the tinny speakers that lie on our chests, carrying the distorted chatter from the TVs above our beds.

The next day, one by one, we go down to theatre. Kevin first, then it's my turn. The weird filmic angle of ceilings tracking past as the barouche rolls along the corridors, then the cliché of the wide circular lights, the men and women in face masks and rubber boots – you think 'slaughterhouse', 'meatworkers', can't help it. Then the pleasant sedative and the big knockout you don't even remember coming. The next thing is a bright recovery ward, a voice, and an arm wrapping your arm with a pressure belt. Morphine, the smiling world above the pains and decisions and activities going on all around you. Morphine, like going down a sunlit stream on a lilo. I could easily come to like this stuff too much. I see why they keep it locked away. Though my legs are cut to blazes, I'm enjoying myself. I feel cradled, it all makes glowing sense to me; the hospital system with its rituals and meals and machines, its steel surfaces and pecking orders.

Later pain comes in ripples and wavelets, then surf breaks. The nurse is changing my dressings. Where they have stuck to the wounds, she pours on sterile water to unglue them. The water comes in little packets. She uses about thirty of them, patiently snipping them open and throwing the used plastic away.

'Why don't they give you a bottle of the stuff?' I ask. 'Would save a lot of plastic.'

'We have to throw away the scissors too,' she says.

'You're kidding, one use and you throw good scissors away!'

'Sometimes they're collected for Third World hospitals.'

Kevin stands and fills his urine bottle to the top like a bull pissing.

'Jees that was a good one,' says Tom. All the private functions, urinating, farting, belching, throwing up, we do in front of each other here. A bark of secrecy has been stripped away; we are barer, more raw people. Colin's bed is empty.

'He might still be in recovery,' says one of the nurses.

Lunch, afternoon tea, the newsagent with his stand on a trolley, then the night shift comes on. Still no sign of Colin. An orderly is tidying up his stuff, putting it away in blue hospital bags. A man is reduced to these things: a toothbrush and a pair of slippers. We finally winkle it out of one of the night nurses. Colin had a cardiac arrest after surgery. They couldn't start his heart again. The three of us resume our small tasks and diversions, taking furtive glances at each other – survivors. The sun has already gone down and the grey, watery light begins to seep from the windows of the ward.

Tide: My Father's Dementia

Sleepless tonight. The Richmond River
laps the foot of my bed and trawlers
blazing light come muttering home,
radios arcing from wheelhouse to pillow.
Old Ballina oystermen know the way
to work these tides into luminous gain,
but how do I, thoughts closed tight
around his gathering loss?
What can stay? Something willed
from love and words and time
whispers from the shore
and in the curtains' dance.
A tide washes over his rippled brain,
makes the estuary without him tomorrow.

My Father at the Clothesline

Concentrating on each peg, mouth open,
aghast at the rate the world is leaving him.
His dignity, as he folds his clothes.

Winter Light

In memoriam Jeff Ladd

Rain, fog, grief – bare-limbed
funeral weather. So many signs:
their wedding photo fell from the bench
and the glass shattered.
A raven, glossy black and blue-eyed
appeared under the lemon tree, then
tipped over the bird bath he'd put there.
The list of missing tiles from the scrabble set
I, D, R, O, noted in his neat hand,
and placed in the box.
So methodical. So hopeless
against the great forgetting.

Mists, sun-showers, rainbows;
light in the green of the deep winter hills.
Following the old stream, still partly there
like a secret room in the life of the suburb.
Appearing again over familiar rock,
making the same gurgles and rills among
the shrieking birds, their breathy wings.

I look down into the stream where
he will neither go, nor stay.
Atoms in the gold tannic water,
smoke in the Blackwood winter air.

Pantuns in the Orchard

Sunset. In the still, intensely humid air, the insect and bird sounds increase, the swallows make their last swoops over the pond, and the bats come out to hunt in the orange sky. The *bilals* from the three local mosques begin their overlapping songs for *maghrib*, the evening prayer. One of the prayer-singers has a lovely voice, but the other two rasp away and we wish their loudspeakers would short circuit. The five daily prayers, starting at dawn, keep the hours for us here in this clock-less house.

We are living in a two-storey kampong house, the Rumah Uda Manap. It is over a hundred years old and was moved here piece by piece from the banks of the Perak River and restored. The wooden building has a belian-shingled roof and hand-carved scrollwork between the walls and the high ceilings. Internal and external panels are carved with Chinese motifs of fruit, flowers and birds, and painted with the original lime-wash colours of beautiful ochres, blues and greens. The house sits amongst trees laced with congea vines at the back of the Rimbun Dahan estate.

Rimbun Dahan means 'laden bough', and is the home of Angela and Hijjas Kasturi. Located about forty kilometres north-west of Kuala Lumpur, it was once an orchard, growing mangoes and durians. It is now a fourteen-hectare garden, a private house, an art gallery and several studio spaces and dwellings generously loaned to visiting artists from Australia, Indonesia, Malaysia and other parts of the world.

I am staying here with my wife, the artist Cathy Brooks. Cath is gathering materials for artworks based on patterning in Muslim architecture and script, traditional fabric design and natural forms and objects found around the Rimbun estate and on the village roads. I'm researching the traditional Malaysian poetic form, the pantun, and writing some contemporary pantuns of my own. My source book, lent to me by Angela Kasturi, is a lemon-yellow edition of *Pantun Melayu*, edited by R.J. Wilkinson and R.O. Winstedt and published by Malaya Publishing House in Singapore in 1957.

There are many types of pantun: the pantun *budak-budak* for children, the pantun *berkaseh sayang* for lovers, and the pantun *berkait*, the chained pantun imported into Western literature as the 'pantoum', where the second and fourth lines of the preceding stanza become the first and third of the next.

I'm more interested in the pantun *tunggal* or 'single' pantun. It has four iambic lines with an *a b a b* rhyme scheme. The first two lines (called the *pembayang*) draw their imagery from the outside world: nature, farming, and village life, and the last two lines (the *maksud*) turn inward toward human relationships and psychology. *Pembayang* means 'hint' or 'atmosphere' and *maksud* means 'point' or 'purpose'. The connection between the pairs of lines is sometimes obvious, sometimes not. These pantuns function in a similar way to proverbs, riddles, and epigrams. It is not only the brevity and simplicity of the form that attracts me, but the mental motions it embodies; outward to observe the natural world, inward to the mind, then out again to perceive the connection between the two.

Before leaving Australia I was told by Malaysian scholar Raimy Che-Ross that the pantun is still very much a living popular form in Malaysia, used for intimate private correspondence, and, more publicly, during wedding speeches, by politicians in parliament, in student jousts (like a rap battle) and as the basis for pop songs. I decide to test out its currency on the Rimbun Dahan estate. Maznah, the gardener's wife, says she knows pantuns but is too shy to recite them to me. So is Siti, the cook from the big house. Anum, the gallery manager, is more forthcoming. She recites from memory this traditional pantun:

Kalau ada sumur di ladang,
Boleh hamba menumpang mandi?
Kalau ada umur yang panjang,
Boleh kita berjumpa lagi?

Her quick translation is:

If there's a pond in the field
may I take a bath?
If I live long enough
can we meet again?

The veiled eroticism of bathing in this person's pond in the *pembayang*, with its natural external imagery, then the deepened meaning, the personal psychological one, which the *maksud* makes clear, means this pantun is, in effect, a proposal of love. They are naughty but nice, this species of pantun. You can ask if you have a future together by saying 'can I have a dip in your paddock?' – very useful in the modest and highly circumscribed Muslim Malay culture.

Anum also tells me that she found several pantuns when looking through a box of old love letters written by her parents in their courting days. A standard finish to their letters was:

Pecah kaca,
pecah gelas.
Sudah baca,
 harap balas.

Break mirror,
break glass.
After reading,
hope reply.

This sort of pantun is used in a formal way; the first two lines employed to achieve the rhyme are not always consequential.

Another example mentioned by Winstedt in *Pantun Melayu* is where a moral message is carried simply by mentioning four kinds of fish:

Siakap, senohong,
gulama, ikan diri.

Because this rhymes with:

Berchakap pun bohong,
lama-lama menchuri.

Which means, 'If you start by lying, you'll end by stealing', but this second half is often left unsaid. An English equivalent might be something like 'sticks and stones will break my bones' where the message of the completing rhythmic line is so well known we don't need to voice it.

Some pantuns are rather heavily loaded with proverbial wisdom, but others have a lighter touch, and a joy in natural atmosphere. In this aspect, they are similar to haiku. They can also be delightfully erotic. Henri Fauconnier, a rubber planter turned writer, gives this pantun in his 1930 novel *Malaisie*:

Kerengga di-dalam buloh,
serahi berisi ayer mawar.
Sampai hasrat di-dalam tuboh
 tuan sa-orang jadi penawar.

Red ants in the hollow of a bamboo,
Vessel filled with essence of roses.
When lust is in my body
only my love can bring me appeasement.

No one knows the exact age of the pantun form. Raimy Che Ross told me that evidence from engravings on tombs suggests it goes back to at least the thirteenth century. Its earliest appearance in manuscript in the *Sejarah Melayu* dates from the beginning of the seventeenth century. The pantun first appeared in English through the writings of the British colonialist Sir Stanford Raffles and William Marsden's *Grammar and Dictionary of the Malay Language*, published in 1812. The pantun *berkait* was later imported into French via a letter from the children's author Ernest Fouinet to Victor Hugo, which contained an example called 'Pantoum Malais'. Hugo published it in 1829 in his book *Les Orientales – Odes et Ballades*. Charles Baudelaire further popularised the pantoum, publishing his own, *Harmonie du Soir*, in 1857. Twentieth-century and contemporary poets such as Donald Justice, John Ashbery, Carolyn Kizer and our own John Anderson, Lorin Ford and Jordie Albiston have used the linked pantun in their work.

But back to the pantun *tunggal* – the 'single' pantun. My aim is to write one per day. Four good concentrated lines. In this task I often fail. Some days nothing comes, on others I write three pantuns, to discover the next day that not one of them is worth keeping. They are small poems, but risky. Because they have a rhyme scheme and a beat (which I admit I only follow loosely) but especially because the *maksud* insists you say something compact about the human condition, you always walk on the edge of the trite, the too-neat summation.

In setting a daily target, I work with what comes to hand in the house and around the Rimbun estate: the pond and the way microcosms of water gather in the bowls of the lotus leaves after a rain storm, a dizzy gecko landing next to my writing table a few moments after I turn on the overhead fan, a bobbing dove snapping the branch on which it stands with its mate, the roadside fires the locals light every sunset ...

But then other, larger events overtake me. Halfway through the residency my father dies suddenly. He had been suffering from dementia, but was physically well, and my biggest fear was that after three months away he wouldn't recognise me when I returned. I never expected that I wouldn't see him alive again. We fly back to Adelaide and midwinter grief, cold rain, the funeral, some time with my mother in the family home, then resume our trip. Coming back to this carved wooden house in a tropical garden feels like a false reality, writing little four-lined poems, vain and irrelevant. I have constant dreams just before dawn each day in which my father appears to me and wakes me by calling my name. Eventually, when I can write again, the opening pantun of the sequence grows from this.

The light comes so slowly.
Another hazy, smoky dawn.
Dreams of my dead father woke me early.
There's too much time, then there's none.

The sun is now well down behind the plong trees. Cath and I put our work aside and go out for our evening stroll. Down the road our friend the sculptor Dan Wollmering is sitting at a desk outside his cottage. He is stripped to the waist, quietly working on little cardboard shapes he is sticking together with masking tape. Spread out on the desk is his collection of seedpods and leaves from the local trees that have helped inspire some of the maquettes he is so carefully crafting. Next, we call on another of our new artist friends, Samsudin Wahab, who is just starting for the day. He's a young Malaysian painter who does manga-style oils and linocuts featuring grinning, skull-like self-portraits that are highly satirical and political. Samsudin works all through the night while playing Red Hot Chilli Peppers in his headphones and chain smoking. He targets media, corrupt judges and police, so I show him a pantun on the subject. As well as the *Book of Hours*, I've been working on a group of modernisations from the old *Pantun Melayu*, altering either the *pembayangs* or the *maksuds* so they refer to more contemporary life:

The judge faces the camera and lies.
He's bent what's right.
The law is a black fowl that flies
by night.

It's based on the *Ayam hitam terbang malam* pantun where a 'black rooster flying at night' is used to mean something inscrutable and clandestine.

Samsudin shows us some new ink drawings in which he is morphing humans into objects that symbolise them: a policeman's head becomes a gun, a fat politician fuses with his limousine. Samsudin asks for further suggestions. 'What about a mufti transforming into the bulging dome of his mosque?' I say, but that's off-limits in today's Malaysia, even for Samsudin. His art looks wild, but he's still a good Muslim, doesn't drink, and his girlfriend wears the *tudung* headscarf.

Earlier in the week I had an opportunity to read some of the pantuns to an audience of young Malaysian architecture students when they came to visit the Rimbun estate and art gallery. Standing in front of ominous bitumen paintings by Jalaini Abu Hassan depicting cleared hillsides and burnt-out forests, I tried out a handful of pantuns. The erotic and the environmental ones seemed to get the strongest reaction:

Oil palms, oil palms, oil palms, oil palms.
Freeways, freeways, freeways, freeways.
Oil palms, oil palms, oil palms, oil palms.
Smoke-haze, smoke-haze, smoke-haze, smoke-haze.

I realise that it is months since we've seen the stars here. It is not only the localised burning of rubbish; there is a permanent haze in the sky and the smell of smoke. We are told, 'It's the Indonesians' – burning the forests of Sumatra, but of course much of the smoke comes from the clearing of land here for the advancing ocean of oil palms.

I think because of all the reports about Malaysia cutting down its own forests and the forests of others, I expected it to be a wasteland with no place for fauna left, but where we live is rich in wildlife. Obviously being in a fourteen-hectare garden helps, but even wandering around the back-roads we see many monkeys in the trees. The estate is home to wrens, pied robins, peaceful doves, kingfishers, squirrels, grey and long-tailed macaques, and there are monitor lizards 'biwah' in the ponds. These look scary (they are much bigger than a goanna and swim very fast) but they are harmless, so we are told. A little bat often flies into the dining room at night while we are eating, and our walls are home to pale, clucking geckos. We also have a visitor we never see, except for its droppings downstairs; the workers here tell us it's a *moosang* – a civet.

Coming back to the house after our walk, the sounds of the night flood in through the open shutters. We want to live in nature, but above it, and yet, in the end, we can't escape being part of it. With the lights off, it is possible to wonder if we are inside, or outside the house. The pantuns shift back and forth between nature and culture; little worlds built in the face of transience. I write about thirty in my time at Rimbun Dahan and decide to assemble some of them into this *Book of Hours*, which starts at dawn and finishes under the mosquito net in the warm, clicking night.

A Book of Hours at Rimbun Dahan

The light comes so slowly.
Another hazy, smoky dawn.
Dreams of my dead father woke me early.
There's too much time, then there's none.

I start the great four-bladed ceiling fan.
Seconds later, a gecko drops to the floor,
stunned. Yes, the world's like that.
We all hang on as long as we can.

In the house of shutters, but no window glass,
the outside world slips across dark-wood mirrors.
Shum hammering in the heat, Siti sweeping the path.
Life in slivers.

Landing next to her, the little male dove
bobs so vehemently on the twig, it snaps.
His need to impress his love
means now they both must flap.

Last night a gecko ate a grasshopper's body
but left its head, still alive this morning, on the floor.
Time eats you like that, but more slowly.
You become a twitching mask of thoughts.

          ∽

Mosquitoes fly out when you shift something black,
whining and hiding again in the room.
Some people I know like to hurry back
to restore themselves in comfortable gloom.

          ∽

That cicada sounds like a dentist,
drilling all day into my eye-tooth nerve.
Shrilling on and on about Time,
everything you love, but can't preserve.

          ∽

The swallows loop back over the pond,
dive and circle, as they must do.
Words repeat in my mind; words
I failed to say when I most needed to.

          ∽

Gathering thunder. The eye of the day
winks smoky orange, slips under
a *tuduk* of purple and monsoon grey.
Add to this drama, the bilal and rooster.

          ∽

Out of the sky of luminous black
rain falls joyfully. You and I
who lived so long alone together
now walk again under one umbrella.

∾

The lotus leaves hold silver discs,
small worlds of water above the pond.
Why did I think my circle so small
and nothing beyond?

∾

The wren in the dripping congea vine
flutters off water from the storm.
Our ceiling leaked; on the floor puddles shine.
Resilient, in the after-light, the quiet forms.

∾

The sour smoke of roadside fires,
rubbish smoulders at end of day.
Old needs, hopes half-realised,
and something else we threw away.

∾

The pattern of the stone path disappears
under a new green *ikat* of moss.
Walking it gives me a change of mood.
Why all this thinking about loss?

∾

Under the mosquito net, settling to sleep,
you feel safe from the world's attacks.
Then you hear the needling, invisible whine
of that one mosquito inside the net; the mind.

From the estate's wall, grey macaques leap
into the laden mango tree.
From your side of the bed, you told me to sleep,
but the night's so warm, and I want something juicy.

Traffik

Next to the Sungai Besi tollgate on the freeway to Seremban, The Student lives in a twenty-storey building of sun-faded grey and pink. He lives out past the wrecking yards, past the unfinished apartments where stray cats and rubbish occupy the floors, past the holey footpaths on which no one walks and that disappear anyway. From the stairwell of his tower block, as he goes up and down each day, he can see a sign: PRESTIGE LIFESTYLE PROJECT that some sharp Kuala Lumpur *agsekutifs* have erected over a gigantic hole in the local clay. Fifty or sixty other apartment buildings, almost identical to his own, fill the horizon.

This afternoon he is receiving instructions on his mobile for a trip he must take to Kota Kinabalu. The phone is so small, it looks like he is simply leaning his head on his hand. As he listens to Middleman's voice, The Student looks down from his seventeenth-floor window to the tollbooth women below, with their uniform headscarves, collecting money from the stream of drivers – all those who don't have electronic tagging yet. Human arms go down for the money, then up. Mechanical arms go up for the cars, then down. Endless, mute.

The Student is twenty-seven years old and halfway through a medical degree. He is Malay, taller than average, with a slight curl to his short black hair. He has only met Middleman once; from then on, everything has been done by mobile phone and electronic bank-transfer. The window lets in a slight breeze, and though you can hear the freeway, it is quiet at this height. A bird, which sounds manufactured, is singing somewhere. Middleman's calm voice ends the call. The Student will have to go into Chinatown, to a *Klinik* on Jalan Heng Likir, where he can buy more anaesthetic with no questions asked.

<hr />

Middleman resides in a white split-level house, with pool and garden, in the quiet back streets of Bangsar. His driveway is lined by frangipanis in flower – odourless, but a brilliant cadmium red.

He is sitting in the front guest room with his new business partner, at an ornate circular table made of blackwood in the Baba Nyonya style, its legs decorated with carvings of herons and mouse deer.

The room is cool and quiet, with little potted ferns and ginger plants in the open windows. Does his wife know what they do? She must. She's there the whole time in the kitchen, making a sour, pungent prawn soup for lunch.

'My account is with BNSB. You should put it here.' Middleman hands over a slip of paper with two rows of numbers. 'You know the ruler of Zimbabwe, Robert Mugabe, has an account with us at BNSB, and he and his wife have holidays here in Malaysia. Yes, at Langkawi Island Resort.'

BNSB is that beautiful bank in central Kuala Lumpur by the filthy, cemented river Klang. So tall and white, decorated with a fine Islamic filigree of stone. Pure, like a mosque.

Middleman is an upper middle manager in BNSB. He wears a light-blue denim shirt and pressed black trousers. He is in his early fifties, hair silver and neatly combed from left to right. His eyebrows are still black. His ancestry is Peranakan, a Chinese-Malay family from Penang. He has smile wrinkles and very good, white teeth.

'There is a change of plan. I have heard they will be checking the cargo of the logging ship. So we will go differently. We will use hand luggage. A student I know. He's reliable. His course is expensive.'

In Chinatown, The Student walks out of the Pasar Seni station into the light. There is an echoing, cracking sound. Is someone breaking crates? Is it fireworks? No. Shotguns. Four men in city uniform, dark blue, beside the concrete columns of the light rail overpass, are shooting crows out of the sky. Onlookers stand beside the gunmen, watching the cawing, confused, black birds. Crack! Crack! A crow dives into the pavement in front of The Student, flutters sideways on one ruined wing. There are three more dead in the gutter and one on the windscreen of a parked car, like a big black ticket. Crack! Crack! He sees the recoil impact the men's shoulders. More wounded and unwounded birds in the sky. Why do they stay circling and cawing? An Indian woman with a crimson sari and butter-yellow parasol walks in front of him, the colours so intense in the sun they start to burn the eye and dissolve.

~∞~

The special lighting is already on in the secret room in the apartment in Shinjuku. Outside, Tokyo city is busy with night traffic, the bars, the late workers emerging from quieter subways, the golden empire lighting of the DoCoMo against the skyline. A thunderstorm is boiling up black clouds unnoticed above the hermetically sealed apartment block.

Morii is thirty-two years old. He has never had a girlfriend, or hired some comfort. He does not like human touch, except, perhaps, his own. He steps in from the sterile, subtly perfumed air of the corridor to his scrupulously clean and sparsely furnished apartment. He follows Shorui Awaremi no Rei: compassion and kindness to all living things. He is a Buddhist and a vegetarian.

Morii is also a rich young man. He has an exceptional ability to design very specialised and very small electronic components. Some of the latest mobile phones do what they do because of him, or at least partly – it seems it is a business of almost telepathic co-invention.

Morii's apartment, because of its Shinjuku address and size, would cost half a million yen per month to rent, but he owns it outright.

His mother lives in Ota. His father died in a subway accident when Morii was twelve. There was no suggestion it was suicide, though he was a businessman who lost badly in the crash of '89. Merely distraction. Reading something on top of his briefcase, he stumbled off the platform as the train arrived. Now Morii takes the same Yamanote line a few stops to Meguro where he works, passing each day through the Shibuyu station where it happened.

Morii has an older brother he hardly sees, who lives in Yamaguchi with his wife and children. His mother is not particularly worried that Morii has no intention to marry. For her, he remains the baby of the family. She likes that he visits so often, bringing exquisite gifts for her: traditional wooden dolls, papers, porcelain.

At the entrance of Morii's apartment there is a crowded little kitchen on the right with barely enough room to pivot between the cupboards and the stove. A similarly compressed bathroom and laundry are on the left. Ahead is a Western-style room with a round coffee table, a few chairs, and a couch that is also a fold-out bed near the window. Behind a shoji screen there is what would normally be Morii's bedroom, but he has given this up for the secret room, so he sleeps on the couch. His clothes and shoes are in an open closet. Morii dresses beautifully in suits of Australian super merino wool, styled in Italy. He takes a set of folded overalls from a box beside the couch-bed, and goes to the tiny bathroom to change.

The atmosphere of his apartment so high up here is subdued; there are a few photos of his family, and one of his graduation on the wall. There is a small library of Japanese titles that look like specialist tomes of some kind. The distant headlights of cars on the freeway approaching this part of the city look like twin white fireflies slowly descending the drawn white blinds in a lazy S, swinging out, then in, then down, to disappear.

Inside the bathroom Morii slips off his grey silk tie, puts his suit jacket and trousers on a hanger, and dresses in the rust brown overall. Tonight he also puts on a paper face mask because at work this afternoon one of his colleagues went home sick. He must be careful. Morii goes to the shoji screen at the partition. Inside is another wall, with a sliding door leading to a glass airlock. Before going into the secret room, he stops and looks back over his shoulder at the world outside the window, thinking, All this ugliness. Why shouldn't I have something beautiful?

In Kota Kinabalu two shirtless boys come through the gap in the galvanised-iron fence around the building site. They've walked from the besser block shanties, through the field with the concrete tunnels overgrown with dark, densely leafed vines. Now they step into the bulldozed space where other shanties like theirs once huddled. It is a grey-and-white rectangle of compressed rubble and stones, awaiting a new shop-lot or commercial *kompleks* or hotel. So much newly constructed space – who fills it, and with what? The two boys, one in white shorts, one in black, run into this emptiness, where at least they can fly a kite. Theirs is homemade from a square of pink plastic and the string is wrapped around a water bottle pulled from the garbage. The kite works, works for free. Picked up by the wind at dusk, it flies above the angle of the new shopping centre rooftop, even (it seems to them) above the height of the big hotels. The boys run barefooted over the compacted rubble where sparrows hop because even here, some food, some hope, may be found. They fly their kite back and forth until darkness and the warm rain sends them home to the hovels for who knows what dinner in the single-bulb rooms where the heat lies still. And the fluorescent lights come on in the new air-con hotels and the bank BNSB lights up red above the empty floors.

On his way to the airport, The Student sees the pink kite from his taxi window, but not the boys, hidden by the fence. He keeps his large carry-on bag in his lap. The Chinese taxi driver tried to take it from him and put it in the boot but he wouldn't let him. Now the driver talks too much. He has crooked teeth and barks rapidly about the city's problems. The front of his taxi is cluttered with a Buddha, a toy orang-utan, Chinese gods, fans, medallions, and ancestor worship cups. All these old things The Student has left behind. He's convinced the world does not work this way. Perhaps he should have taken the bus, but he doesn't want any extra waiting. No costly delays.

'You should have left more time. Must be two hours before the flight.'

'I've checked-in electronically. Only carry-on bags. No problem.'

'You go to Japan?'

'Japan, yes.'

'Japan good place. People work hard, not like here, lazy.'

The Student turns away and looks out the window at the passing shop-lots and already decaying five-storey apartments, the concrete stained and eaten by the tropics.

If he can be a doctor he will have a great car and live in a nice house in KL, and he will care for people. He doesn't have a rich family to pay for his tuition. His father is like this man. He drives a taxi around Sungai Buloh late at night for a lousy five ringgit a ride. That will not be The Student. It is enough for his father, with his little banana and okra patch jammed in by the railway line at the back of the terrace houses, but it is not enough for him. He will be a doctor and it will be a great car like a Range Rover.

Two direct flights each week, Kota Kinabalu – Tokyo.

At the airport branch road the billboard says A SHOPPING MEGAMALL IN BORNEO! The mascot, a rainforest creature, computer cute. Nothing like a real animal, but generated from tests on human perceptions of friendly eyes, happy mouth, funny nose. A SHOPPING MEGAMALL IN BORNEO! Dropping back in the taxi window. Flight times – Englishmalay echo, incomprehensible. Ancillary income. Logos in the glass. The advertising on cups, seats, trays, toilet mirrors. No place your eye can rest without being subject to promotion. The bored girls selling the same designer watches and sunglasses, the same perfume, alcohol and chocolates. Cold, cold ranks. Global glitter. Local girls, just out of high school, last bus home, or their fathers pick them up from the turnoff. Shop girls wanted. Must have good English, able to work to eleven every night.

~⬦~

The Student must take the queue to the right, where the guard sits by himself. It would be disastrous to be made to join the left-hand queue where the two women in headscarves and navy-blue uniforms watch over the machine. He glances nervously at the soldier between the queues, avoiding eye contact. No, it's all right, no one will stop him proceeding into the right-hand lane towards the grey cream cube.

Awas! Rapiscan. Radiation Hazard. The bored

middle-aged security guard watches the carry-on bags progress. Those strange colours (like old polaroids) of the repetitive luggage interiors: clothes, books, sunglasses, phones, tubes of toothpaste, face cream, and lotions, now gathered in clear zip-lock bags. Occasionally something that requires stopping. A pair of scissors they must lose. A stupid souvenir *kris* – they are forgetful some people. Something with wires or batteries. Just a tape recorder. One absent-minded woman's vibrator – he did not stop the conveyor belt or look at her. A good Muslim man, he did not want to inspect this. Why didn't she put it in baggage, this thoughtless Westerner?

The pay is very poor and the job is boring and Middleman arranges some extra income for him. He knows The Student will be coming through tonight. Ah yes, there he is now. When the big brown bag goes through, he sees it there, under the folded shirts, like a little burial. The X-ray goes right through to the skeleton, so like the bones of a human baby. *Awas.* Kawasan. Sinar-X. Rapiscan. Carry on.

As Morii closes the shoji screen behind him and goes through the airlock, there is a musty animal smell. There is muted green light from tinted overhead bulbs and a looped soundtrack of forest insects and birds.

She moves forward on a rope suspended from the ceiling and swings into Morii's arms. She is happy to see him home from work. He changes the day-night cycle so they can be together.

Morii goes to a chest-sized portable fridge at the side of the room. He puts her down to sit on the floor while he unlocks the fridge. He has to keep it locked because she is very clever. Morii draws out a basket of fruits and places it on the floor in front of her. She begins carefully selecting and eating each one.

Mango, durian, jackfruit, lychee, fig, mangosteen, banana – he must get these every two days from the markets. Also tree bark. Difficult to find. There are only two pet shops in Tokyo for this type of bark. Also live insects. Crickets. Worms. This is much easier, just like feeding a pet frog. Also bamboo shoots, and raw eggs. He eats what she eats, except for the bark and worms.

They are a pair, there on the floor in the secret green room, Morii's rust-brown overall matching her fur. He squashes the black skin of a mangosteen and picks out the sweet pearly flesh from the womb-like red interior. Her lips curve out for the delicacy as he feeds it to her by hand. She has weak-black-coffee eyes set close together in round craters, a snub nose and a smiling up-turned mouth in a very round foro faco, with soft bay whiskers at the edge. A high polished forehead, with wispy upswept hennaed hair, like a balding old woman.

Akiko (he has given her his mother's mother's name) is now three years old.

She came to him as a baby. Now she eats everything,

not just milk. In the forest she would be carried by her mother until she was four years old, so to her Morii is her mother.

꩜

Now The Student must put the big brown bag in the overhead locker, and he knows it just fits, because he's done this before. He made sure he was at the head of the line-up when it was boarding time. He wants his bag right next to him, right above his head. The smell is a cause for concern. He washes them first, but they can still smell strong. He hopes people think it is his own body odour. Once a woman next to him in the exit queue held a handkerchief to her nose. He looked at her and she didn't make eye contact again. And then there's the anaesthetic – sagatal. Too little and they wake up; too much and they never wake up again. Lucky he's a trainee doctor. But it still goes wrong. They are delicate. Last time a whole trip to Japan for nothing. All they pay then is one third. Take out the cost of the tickets and he has almost nothing. On the fringes of the BTC logging concessions on the upper Kinabatangan, or over the border in Kalimantan, the villagers get a thousand ringgit for each one. That's only three hundred dollars. In Tokyo they sell them for one hundred times that. He's taking the biggest risk. He should get more. He's heard of others carrying two at once. Dangerous, but if you lose one, you still have the other to sell. This is a budget overnight flight and they make you pay extra if you want a blanket and pillow. He should get more.

⁓

In the New Love bar in Kota Kinabalu a man from Borneo Timber Corporation swaggers onto the tiny stage, grabs the microphone from the Filipina singer and bellows his own version of the song very badly, distorting the PA. The baron from BTC uses the band as his own personal karaoke, because this is his town. The Filipina singer wearing long black eyelashes and a dress of cerise sequins stands back smiling but insulted. She leans on the drum machine and pats her big black hairdo and waits. She waits patiently for her rightful place to be returned to her, singing love songs to the shadowy drinkers. When the BTC baron finishes there will be false applause and she will gracefully take back the microphone damp from his spit and smile and sing again. The men from BTC will laugh loud as the baron collapses back in his chair and they will slap him on the back because this is also their town. BNSB is financing BTC's expansion of its logging operations in Sabah and Sarawak, and internationally in West Kalimantan. The Borneo News says that stories about the destruction of orang-utan habitat in the international media are negative, misleading and absolutely fabricated. *The proclamation of Totally Protected Areas are further proof to dispel reckless claims of oil palm plantation*

and logging versus the orang-utan habitat loss when all
areas are listed as totally protected areas which are off
limits to commercial or industrial use, said the forestry
commission.

Morii has no respect for people who buy rare pets
only to show off. He knows a businessman who paid
one million yen for a giant stag beetle. What for? Ugly
creature. The man puts it in a glass case for a party to
show his friends. Then he forgets about it. He has no
compassion for the animal, and it cannot show feelings,
like Akiko. Morii tells himself that many people talk
about the destruction of the rainforests, but they do
nothing. 'I am doing something. I am protecting Akiko.
She is an orphan. Her forest is gone – just oil palms
now. She will die there without me.'

Before he faces customs, The Student takes the brown
bag with him into the men's toilets, and locks the door
of the cubicle. He unzips the bag and parts the shirts.
The small fuzzy chest appears still at first and he has a
moment of panic, but he holds the back of his hand over
the nostrils, and there, reassuringly, is the tiniest breeze.
From down in the bag he takes out his stethoscope,
given to him so proudly by his father who worked thirty
nights in the taxi to buy it. The little heartbeat is slow
but strong enough. He could walk now straight through

the 'Nothing to Declare' gate, but this is too risky. A random search could ruin everything. In the past he could have gone to 'Items to Declare' and been taken down for an interview with the customs men.

He has done it before this way with false paperwork. Importing monkeys into Japan is legal. They are used for experiments, and there was a time when the customs men could not tell a baby orang-utan from a baby rhesus. But new laws have been passed by the Diet, education programs brought in. Now they must pay the cleaner.

The Student waits two, three, five minutes for the knock on the door. He is tired. It was a long flight with no sleep. Why doesn't the cleaner come? He knows he's out there because they nodded to each other when he went in. Being careful perhaps, waiting for an empty room.

At last there is the knock on the door. The Student carefully places the baby on the closed toilet seat, wrapped in a T-shirt. He goes to wash his hands. The cleaner enters and places the baby in his own bag. He is just finishing his night shift, and on his way home he will make a detour to the back room of a suburban pet shop.

With clean hands and a normal bag, except for a faint musty smell amongst the shirts, The Student proceeds to immigration and customs. He will state his purpose as 'business', stay one night in a cheap hotel, and return to KL. Middleman will credit his account. He walks through the same displays of watches and sunglasses, the same perfume, alcohol and chocolates that he left in Kota Kinabalu. In the refrigerated, glittering shops, largely deserted, the shopgirls stand, this time, Japanese.

～∞

When Akiko is content, she pushes aside the fruit basket with her feet and puts her arms around Morii's neck. He stands, swinging her up onto his hip, in baby carrying position. In four more years Akiko will be fully grown. What then? She will look like a small woman with hennaed hair, rough cut from her bulging forehead. She will weigh fifty kilos and be much stronger than him. What will he do with her then, with her long levering arms, her toes curving round like fingers, her brown watery eyes staring at him, and teeth that could tear his hand off at the wrist?

Morii places Akiko on her rope swing in the green light. The swing hangs from a wooden platform built on top of a thick bamboo pole. The platform is also made from bamboo, a weave of canes, making a messy nest. He worries that she is missing others of her species, but consoles himself that when mature, in nature, they are solitary. There may be some trouble when she reaches puberty, but he thinks there is no reason she cannot live here her whole life. That could be fifty years. Fifty years in one secret room in a Shinjuku apartment.

Morii has heard talk of a 'ghost mother' standing behind every baby, but he chooses not to believe it about Akiko. 'She was already an orphan. They did not have to kill her mother to take the baby away from her. Akiko was found wandering at the edge of the logging road, so her mother must have been already dead. They saved her. And now I am her only family.' This is what he tells himself. Morii begins sweeping up a pile of droppings under the bamboo platform. The pattern of bird calls loops on the soundtrack; an emerald dove's low coos, followed by the high-pitched trills of a sunbird.

Tangled fronds and spirals like Oran Ulu art. The forest edge. The green wall beside the new BTC logging road. Rough-barked meranti, stripy janggau, the kandis and ulin draped and tangled and wound with ferns and epiphytes. Inside, behind the green wall, an upholstery of moss by still, golden pools. An absence of bird calls, even the cicadas silent. The hunters with the tranquilliser darts, silent too.

When the call comes from Middleman, The Student is sitting in an open-walled Chinese restaurant to the side of the Night Market. He is eating a bowl of mee soup, simple and cheap, but delicious. Maghrib. The sun has just set and the bilal's voice floats over the district from Masjid Jamek. Crows, survivors of the flock the blue-uniformed men had been shooting last month, fly overhead, undefeated, banking and cawing before finding their roosts for the night. As he listens to Middleman's voice, The Student watches the gliding black shapes against the dirty yellow sky, his spoon paused above his soup bowl. It is going to rain, the air so close it will only take a tiny increase in humidity for the whole sky to turn into water.

There is enough noise in the restaurant to keep the call private. Middleman would not leave news like this in a text message. SIM cards are such a hazard. He speaks with his usual calm matter-of-factness. 'We are stopping more exports to Japan. Your trip is cancelled. We will have to find temporary storage for our merchandise.' Two hours ago, Japanese police raided a pet shop in outer suburban Tokyo. They confiscated a baby orang-utan, two proboscis monkeys, eclectus parrots and several rare reptile species. They arrested the owner and seized his client records.

The Student watches the compressed mass of human beings in the Pasar Seni, shoulder to shoulder, working their way between the food stalls where every kind of creature is on sale for them to eat. Rainbow lanterns are coming on, and flashing fairy lights. He watches the green neon feet of the Putra Reflexology Klinik pulsing on and off across the street. Left foot, right foot. The rain comes. The fat, hot drops switching on as if from a showerhead, then quickly forming a wall of water. How will I pay for next year's tuition? was all he thought as Middleman ended the call. It was going well. Only a few more trips. Water begins pooling in the plastic awnings above the food stalls. Behind the stalls, whole pink quails are plunged into cauldrons of boiling oil, tofu and *pisang goreng* are deep-frying. He wonders briefly what would happen if the roof water tipped into that? The Student finishes his soup, then joins the swirling Night Market crowd, disappearing in the hot, wet darkness.

∾

The police, accompanied by the Wildlife Service criminal unit, raid Morii's apartment. Although Morii meekly unlocks the secret room for them and tries to reach Akiko first, the excited officers spring at her, and she retreats to the top of her bamboo nest, shaking the canes and baring her teeth in a half squeak, half scream. Morii attempts to quieten her, but can't in the crowd of raised voices. Why have they brought so many people?

He begins to cry when one of the men climbs up the pole and wrenches Akiko down. She reaches out to Morii with a long, orange-haired arm as two men struggle to wrap her in a restraining cloth and carry her out of the green light into the harsher white light of the living room.

'Please let me carry her to the station,' he begs, but they will not even consider it. Perhaps they are thinking of the newspapers tomorrow; a picture of the Wildlife Service in decisive action mode.

Morii is to be prosecuted. He may have good intentions, but he is part of the problem. It is his demand, and the demand of those like him, that creates the trade.

The judge believes him to be a naive young man. In

his trial it is obvious how idealistic he is. His lawyer presents him as misguided and eccentric but not deserving of a criminal record. There is no jail sentence, only a fine of three hundred thousand yen, which is a very small amount to Morii. The shame is harder to live with, and there is a problem at work because of the publicity. Some of his colleagues make jokes about his 'ape-wife'.

Morii changes jobs to where they do not know him. This means working outside his field of greatest expertise, in a lower, more uninteresting position. Instead of research, Morii now works as a technical supervisor for the production department of a factory making electronic navigation equipment. At night he comes home to the empty secret room, the soundtrack silenced now. Akiko has been sent back with other confiscated animals to an orang-utan rehabilitation centre in Borneo.

Morii takes down the specialised equipment, changes the lighting to normal white, and moves his bed into the room. Perhaps he should buy a saltwater fish tank – one of those large ones with living coral and real anemones and all kinds of bright fish. That would be beauty too, but cool and reasonable beauty. Beauty without too much emotion. Morii has a photo album of Akiko's two years with him. He looks through it most nights.

'It is no great loss,' says Middleman to Business Partner, sipping his cup of water-lily tea, and watching the steam curl into the air-conditioned room. 'There are plenty more clients all over the world. The rich have always loved private zoos. We will bide our time, and find another way to Japan.'

On the walls he has some abstract paintings by contemporary Malaysian artists, and beside him, an antique Chinese screen carved with animals: the bat for happiness, deer for high status, crane for longevity, and the phoenix for rebirth. 'We still have our friend, high-up in Perhilitan, and we are diversified – reptiles and birds are small unit returns but there are many of them.'

He pours more tea. 'I read the strangest article last week in the newspaper. It was called *Escobar's hippos gunned down in Colombia*. After the cocaine boss Pablo Escobar was killed, his collection of animals was divided up between state zoos, but some of his hippos escaped and began to live and breed in the Magdalena River. Imagine it, a troupe of wild hippos in South America! They shot them because they were dangerous to the local people.' He sips his tea, then looks up to make eye contact.' If I had known who the final buyer was at the time, I never would have sold to him. He wanted a large male orang-utan, the agent in Colombia. It ended in Escobar's private zoo. If I had known, I would not have made this sale. I hate drug-dealers. Our government is right to execute them.'

At Sepilok, a small group of orang-utans have come out of the forest to the tree platform, where the men in overalls distribute food from blue plastic buckets. The group comprises one fully grown male and five young females. Below the platform are more than one hundred tourists, chattering and clicking. Morii ignores the inane poses, the groups of locals and foreigners pointing fingers to the sky in peace salutes. He looks straight through them. He wishes they would be silent. They have been told to be silent, but it seems they are unable to stop talking, even when an English woman makes a loud shushing noise and holds her finger to her lips in frustration.

They are lucky today. It is not every day the orang-utans come out of the forest, especially now it is high fruiting season. The ticket seller at the registration centre knows Morii on sight. The quiet Japanese man has been coming everyday for the last week. 'Very unusual to see the same visitor more than once here. They come for the day to tell their friends back home they have seen the orang-utan, but this one is very dedicated.'

Morii has seen her and he is sure she has seen him. If only they would let him get closer to the platform, he is certain she would reach down for him.

Gasoline Flowers

Mohamed Bouazizi,
wanting living space
and a little justice,
became an orange-yellow orchid

Tich Quang Duc,
a wavering lotus of flame

Palden Choetso – a smoky iris,
deadly bright at its centre.

For his land of snow
and a spinning prayer,
Tsering Tashi was a gaping petro hibiscus.

The Museum of Memory, Santiago de Chile

For Raul Zurita and Juan Garrido-Salgardo

The Mapocho hurries to the sea

there is electricity in the iron bed

the snow smells like polished metal

100,000 students are on the streets

the howl that came out of me did not sound human

the shantytown's tree turns white

I was bleeding from my nipples

the students' hair is wet with snow

the river is really just a mountain stream

120 V

< >

240 V

and from my vagina

Neruda died then

the umbrella vendors arrive with the snow

do you ever want to see your children again?

the faces of the student leaders on television

$$- 1.5$$
$$- 1 \qquad - 2$$
$$.5 \qquad\qquad - 2.5$$
AMPERES

the river is always in a hurry

do you ever want to sleep with your wife again?

they have learnt not to trust the cameras

his breathing became more and more hoarse

GENERAL ELECTRIC

the march was peaceful

there was nothing on the world news

the snow smells clean

the river hurries

the bed is wired

Breakfast in Valparaiso

I get up at dawn to walk to the docks. I want to record the sound of the port of Valparaiso as it wakes. As soon as I step into the street, a large black-and-white dog of indeterminate breed, patterned like a Friesian cow, begins to follow me. I stop to check his intentions. He cocks his head and looks back at me with one blue eye and one brown. I'm not sure if he can see through the blue eye, which is cloudy with a slight opalescence. He's not aggressive, just quietly determined to follow me, and so we set off together down the steep, empty streets, with the gulls circling overhead in the first light.

We descend Cumming Street to the Plaza Anibal Pinto, dodging the early communal busses on Condell, then turn directly towards the sea at Melgarejo. I walk fast, paying no attention to his progress, but when I turn around he's still there, a few paces behind, or at intersections close at heel, waiting to cross when I do.

At the Avenida Errazuriz, the port traffic is already heavy and I make a dash for the median strip and then over. When I look back across the road, he's sitting on the other side, perhaps unwilling to step onto such a busy highway, or perhaps this is the edge of his territory. I'm neither happy nor unhappy about us parting company here, and I stride on towards the Sotomayor. A few minutes later I look behind and there he is again, keeping up with the trailing edge of my shadow.

We reach the water, calm today, with the smell of diesel mixing with the brine of the great blue Pacific rolling all across the world to Chile. I stop to listen and so does the dog: gulls, the distant whine of the container terminal, a very quiet slapping of water against the line of fishing boats moored a little way out from the wharf.

Zeus, Estrella, Santa Maria.
Orion, Anita, Julia Rosa.
Maritza, Fernanda, Vaca Loca.
VAL. VALPO. VALPARAISO.

'*Vaca Loca*', 'Crazy Cow', that's what I could call this dog with his Friesian coat and one strange blue eye, except he's the opposite of crazy; quiet, patient and determined to be my companion, showing me that hopeful smile we can't help reading into the faces of dogs.

Down a bit to the left I think will be the best place to record, out of any traffic and sheltered from the wind. But will this dog make unwanted panting or movement? I turn on the recorder and put in my earphones, noticing the distant sounds now in the general field of water, machinery and gulls. There are other, smaller birds, unidentified. Far off are the voices of the sandwich men and sugared peanut sellers setting up for the day, and the peep, peep, peeping of the container terminal as the giant grappling machines reverse. Thankfully, the dog lowers himself down beside my feet and is absolutely silent. We settle in to record.

When you're patient and still, something always happens. I'm in luck. An old man in a rowing boat appears from under the wharf directly below me, unseen till now. In the middle of the boat is a cup holding coins, and two fishermen stand on the stern cross-plank. He rows them nicely across the stereo from right to left, towards the line of fishing boats, making steady oar splashes. An occasional word passes between his passengers. Off they fade into the general acoustic to begin their day's work in the sea.

This is what we recordists hope for; significant auditory events, sounds that when you hear them later without seeing the original scene, still give you the picture. That, and sheer beauty. South America is extraordinarily rich in such events, and here in this part of Chile is a culture that still spruiks and cries out and sings in the streets; musicians, puppeteers, hawkers, barrel organ grinders, unofficial sellers who pack up their goods in a flash and disappear when the inspectors come.

And how's my dog going? He's blinking in the sunshine as it warms his flanks. Smiling again.

The other consideration when recording is when to stop. There will always be more, but you should also be grateful for your luck. I decide that what I have now possesses character and shape, and that to go on would simply be stretching things out.

The dog rises as I turn away from the water. We walk back up to the Plaza Sotomayor where several of his brothers and sisters are sunning away the remnant chill of the night. In Valparaiso the streets belong to the dogs, the rooves to the cats, and the sky to the people. The Valparaisans are like the Venetians, but they build their eccentricities in the air instead of the water. Their soul is steepness and their emblems are the staircase and the stilt.

They prop themselves along the cliff tops and lower themselves down the gully slopes – in sheds, shacks, and wooden houses; multicoloured and multilevelled. Even the bigger homes have something of the precariousness, the perchedness of cubby houses. The people sing and whistle and call each other up from above or down from below, projecting their voices across the gaps. I love this sonic quality of steep towns by the sea.

Spring has come to Valparaiso, with white flares of almond trees here and there, and yellow spurts of Californian poppies in the weeds. There's a renewed optimism in the singing of the canaries and the roaming of the dogs. The sea wind, freezing in the shadows, feels pleasantly refreshing just across the street on the sunny side, where wind chimes and flags record its strength. The street-sellers are spreading their cloths on the footpaths; always something to make, no matter how small.

This city was cobbled together by sailors from all around the world with Crusoean ingenuity. I don't mean down on El Plan with its nineteenth century architectural confections built by the bankers and shipping companies that flourished in Valparaiso until the Panama Canal ended the boom times in 1913. Today these bastions of capital are half-empty and earthquake racked. I mean the *'cerros'*, the eyries and lairs of the heights, hard-won from gravity and the grudging wind.

Now the dog and I progress along the Avenida Esmerelda. It's as though he's appointed himself as my personal guide this morning. I stop at an ATM and he waits outside the glass booth as I withdraw some cash. We go on. Further up the street we come to a shop with its shutter half-open. On the counter inside there are two trays of empanadas, baked not long ago. Now they are cool enough, a woman is transferring them into her display for the morning trade.

Why not? I think, realising what the whole exercise has been about from the beginning. The empanadas are the kind they call *'pino'*, filled with meat, half an egg and a single olive. I tear a *pino* into three and feed it to the dog.

The street dogs of Valparaiso, though inbred, matted and shaggy, appear adequately fed. They are no great nuisance apart from the occasional turd and an irrepressible desire to chase motorbikes. They have their place, and people care for them haphazardly. They sleep in the corners of steps, under shrubbery, and in boxes and abandoned furniture. I don't have a name for this dog, but if he had a name for me it would be *'Desayuno'* – 'Breakfast'.

He continues to follow me, even more enthusiastically, back to the Plaza Anibal Pinto, then up the hill to my door. Ten minutes later, he's still sitting on the front step when I look down through the window, but in another five, he's gone.

Graffiti on the Gates of Paradise

(After William Blake's 1793 etchings)

At length for hatching

Awkward in my body,
I always wanted wings.
With your wise woman's hands
you break me out of my clothes
and all my brittle philosophy.

My son! My son!

Where is he tonight? In the high desert?
In the jaguar forests? Roads of sun, roads of ice.
I pray for him, though I don't know to what.
I pray for him on the mountain bends
and in the cities' alleys.

I want! I want!

I haven't learnt how not to want,
though the doctrines say therein lies peace.
I haven't learnt how not to long,
because that aching gives me life.
This rickety ladder I lean on the moon.

Help! Help!

And who were they to pray to
when they saw no boat on the horizon,
no hand reaching down from the clouds,
only the waves preparing their trench
and hissing 'Siev X, Siev X'?

Aged ignorance

Waiting under my face,
there's an old man who must resist
closing his eyes to the daylight,
must fight the urge to clip his own wings.
The world rubs him closer each day.

O Priest

Professing celibacy
you stole childhoods.
Who can trust your gowns and hats and cloaks?
Now the child believes in fairytales
where the wolf gets away with it.

The traveller hasteth in the evening

The city trees shine with late, illusory gold,
and workers' faces are lit by their mobile phones.
Epicurus says that death can be no worse
than the blankness before we were born.
But sunset quickens me – that foreknowledge of ending.

Gaps

We first see our son sitting on the grass, reading near the Hyde Park fountain, the one with Apollo on top, Diana and Theseus and Aristaeus in the pool below. He arrived before us, so we approach him from a distance through the cathedral of fig trees.

His mother cooees and he stands up for a hug, her first, then me. He's changed; seems taller, leaner, a bit harder. Those same blue eyes are now accentuated by the tanning of his face after two years on the road in South America. His head is shaved on the sides and he has stringy hair long on top; a sort of dreadlocked mohawk. He looks like a character from Avatar, or an escaped minor god from the fountain.

He hadn't told us he was back in the country. He'd wanted to surprise us, but we found out through a panicky friend when he'd asked to stay at her place in Sydney, then disappeared.

We go looking for food and coffee. He tells us he's a vegetarian now, and interested in anarchism. He's been reading *Malatesta*, a book given to him by some travellers he met in Colombia.

He is wearing a grey T-shirt showing lighthouses of America, and brown corduroy pants, bought for a dollar each in Bogota. His feet are shod with second-hand Colombian army boots, the leather worn down to the steel caps on the toes.

'Is that from kicking lefties' heads in jail?' I say.

'Don't joke.'

We walk to Martin Place, find some vegetarian food, then take it back to the café on the edge of the park to talk and eat.

'I haven't seen a television or read a newspaper for two years, so I've got a few gaps. Fill me in on what's been going on here.' What to say? Most of it (the Australian politics in particular) seems like utter trivia. 'So what happened to Rudd?'

'He got a rough deal.'

It sounds so hackneyed when I try to summarise it. The global financial crisis, sub-prime mortgages, spending our way out of it. 'New school buildings – they're everywhere. Your old primary school has a new hall, so does Rosary, and the Murdoch press ran a huge campaign against him for wasteful spending. Then there was the messed-up home insulation scheme, and propaganda from the big mining companies so they didn't have to pay more tax, and his own party didn't like his style anymore ...'

'And the woman, what's she like?'

'OK. Much the same, really.'

The coffee is inky black and good. 'I haven't had coffee like this in a long time.' We wash down the rice balls and nori rolls as ibises scout the park.

'And Obama turned out to be no good?'

'That's not right. He was left so many problems. They're broke. Been spending more than they make for years, and the cost of the Iraq war – a trillion. And he's trying to run a country where people think they're having their freedom taken away from them by introducing a public health scheme.'

I look into his familiar blue eyes (forgotten until today) and he says, 'Did you know the Americans have robot planes they control from game screens? They sit in lounge chairs in these dens and they have a joystick and a screen and they kill real people. And these dens are behind game parlours where kids can come and play and they pick the best ones with the highest scores and give them a job in the killing room.'

'I haven't heard that about the game parlours, but I have seen pictures of the dens where they control the drones. Disgusting. Leather chairs with built-in drink holders.'

He goes on to tell us about the *real politick* of Venezuela and Colombia – the violence and machismo, the double dealing, the military on the streets, the good and bad of socialism. His love for the people he met and his way of life there, surviving on a minimum of money, busking, making things to sell so he could eat, and how the unregulated system works because everyone needs to do it. He made chocolates by hand to sell on the streets of Bogota, but he doesn't like his chances of doing it here. Who would buy one in this park from an unlicensed seller with a cardboard tray?

We missed his nineteenth and twentieth birthdays, though we used Skype a few times – beautiful in its way, but paradoxically distancing, with his moon-shot voice and his image breaking into a pixelated jumble, or frozen to an old photograph eaten by rain and termites. We walk through the Domain and the Botanic Gardens, past the trees hung with bats. An old dragon tree stands out against the sky like a Dr Seuss cartoon. The bats smell musty and so does he, not choosing to wash every day. Down at the quay he says, 'Let's get out of all these tourists,' so we catch the train to Newtown where he's staying for a few nights in a student house.

He's been back in the country for longer than we knew, living up near Newcastle. At Corelli's Café he tells us how he borrowed a bike and went camping on a bush trail for two days, riding under the powerlines on the access tracks into the forest. On the second day, he met another cyclist coming the opposite way. It turned out he was from Spain and our son (now fluent in Spanish) surprised the traveller by asking him in his own tongue what he thought of Australia.

'State control like America with British punctuality.' Our son's heart sank. 'That's how I find it too, coming back.'

And what do I think about it? Heavily regulated, impatient, food-obsessed. A brashness from American media layered on top of English reserve and the old Aboriginal wound, tempered with new Asian and Middle-Eastern influences still working themselves out. Citified, cotton-wool wrapped children, living in more and more virtual worlds. Silently segregated communities. Gated apartment blocks. Somewhere, the traditional self-depreciating humour and outgoing lack of respect like an echo underneath a crumbling, boarded-up pub, bought by developers and soon to be bulldozed.

But I don't say any of this. Just that 'It's true. It's getting more rule-bound here every day. And people get angry really fast if things don't go to plan – but when they do go really wrong, I still think Australians are ready to help each other.'

'Yeah? I was on the beach at Newcastle and I accidently asked something in Spanish – because I'd forgotten the English and these guys told me to go back where I came from. It was pretty funny, really.'

He's hungry again so we order more food. I tell him, 'I'm thinking of going vego too.'

'Do it!'

I used to run a line with myself that it was acceptable to eat a small amount of meat because it was 'natural' for creatures to eat each other, even though we are all sentient beings. And yes, although we are the type of sentient creature that has other choices, if we were aware, and honoured the creature we ate, it was OK. But all that depended on someone, somewhere else, doing the killing. Lately the thought of the process haunted me more and more at table, the industrial lives of so many animals – that, and the increasing discovery of other species' sophistications that we had assumed to be ours alone: tool use, language, deep family bonds …

'Just do it!' he says.

'I'll give it a try.'

Up King Street we look through retro shops – chairs, record players, dining tables, lounges and curtains that were simply the furnishings and fabrics of my (now collectable) childhood. How quickly your own life becomes nostalgia if you let it.

We walk back to Waterloo where we are staying in the apartment of our friend who tipped us off. Just talking quietly, getting to know each other again. The night after we discovered he was back, his mother lost her voice with a throat infection. He jaywalks the intersections while she harries him in a hoarse whisper. He tells her not to be afraid, that bad things happen because fear attracts them. They argue quietly under the trees, mother and son, and I say, 'Yes, but you need some wisdom …'

Our friend buzzes us in to the white-tiled foyer and we go up six floors to her one-bedroom flat. We are sleeping on a fold-down couch in the lounge so we all go out on the small balcony to talk. We look over the lawns in the quadrangle to the thousand other flats. Only three balconies have plants, the others are bare except for BBQs, satellite dishes, some desultory Christmas lights. A lone currawong tries out its call from the top of a cooling tower.

Our son raises one leg of his corduroy shorts and shows us a blue, finely inked tattoo of a wire bicycle above his knee. Next to his left ankle is a triangle of solid indigo. 'My rough play button,' he says. Apart from these, there are no new tattoos or scars.

Sipping tea and eating carrot cake, he fills in a few more gaps.

'One night I was on the street late in Bogota and these four guys came towards me. I could tell it was trouble, so I crossed to the other side of the road, but another two guys jumped out from a corner and suddenly I had two knives against my neck. I told them I only had one mil – that's about fifty cents. They searched me and that's all they found. I told them I wasn't worth robbing. Why not rob the rich instead? But they took it anyway and walked off.

'Then some cops came past on motorbikes. It was straight after it happened, so I pointed out the guys and they chased them down and aimed guns at them. They made them strip and lie down in the street. I wanted revenge so I said they stole fifty mil, but the cops searched them and all they had was my lousy one mil. So I only got my fifty cents back. Six guys and only one mil between them!'

His mother and our friend are making a celebratory meal for him and they send us off to buy wine. We walk up Bourke Street and find a wine shop but decide to keep walking. We take the footbridge over South Dowling Street and the Eastern Distributor, then make our way up through the gum trees at the back of the Moore Park golf course to a high hill where we sit looking at the city skyline. Behind us, men stand in an open-fronted building, driving little white balls into an artificial green paddock.

'Strange species, aren't we?' I say.

'So, how are you?' he asks.

'I'm OK. I like my work, but I'm slowly getting to the point where I want to do something different with my life. I want to maybe go and do something useful somewhere else in the world – like volunteer to teach in Cambodia, or even here – Aboriginal literacy – there's lot's of things I could do. I'm relatively happy, but I feel like I need to connect more directly to people.'

We talk about plans and ideals and commitments and what's stopping me, and I give him some more details about things he's missed: his sister's breakup with her boyfriend, the last days of our family dog, the death of my father. A man with a blue singlet, and tattoos on his huge deltoid muscles, runs up the steep hill we are sitting on, then walks back slowly to the oval below. He repeats the procedure a dozen times. 'He looks like a bouncer – I wouldn't want him chasing me.'

'You'd be the last person I know who'd get into a fight, Dad.'

'I don't know. Somotimes bad stuff just happens.'

'I think nothing happens by chance. I learnt that on the farm in San Agustin. The community leader there told me that bad things happen because you need to learn a lesson from them. It's about energy. If you're full of positive energy and you share that with everyone then nothing bad will come to you. I really believe that.'

'I don't know. It sounds like it presupposes that the universe has some kind of force or deity deciding if you need to learn a lesson or not, or if your energy is positive enough. I think it's more random than that. If there was some kind of controlling justice in the universe, then why did a good, kind man like your pop have such a tortured death?'

'Was it bad?'

'Yes. I'm not going to lie to you. He had twenty days in hell. He was demented. He tore out the drips. Didn't recognise anyone. Didn't drink or eat. He'd signed papers that he couldn't be force-fed or artificially kept alive. Maybe somewhere deep down he knew if he kept tearing out the drips he could die. It was his only way out of the mental pain.'

As we've been talking the sun has slowly gone down behind the city. In the twilight we walk back through the trees towards Bourke Street, passing people exercising their dogs, jogging, shopping, at least half of them talking on mobile phones at the same time. I tell him, 'There's a lot more conversation on the street now than when I was a boy, but most of it is one-ended.' We listen as we carry two bottles of Grenache back to the flat:

'... it's in the red bag near the washing machine ...'

'... I've had enough of your lies ...'

'... yeah, five ninety-nine each ...'

'... no, I said the city end ...'

'... so I told her if you don't do something about it now, you never will ...'

'... the fat ones or the skinny ones ...'

'... and they were doing it in the lounge when I came in ...'

Back at the apartment I turn on the television, which has surprisingly snowy reception for such a new building. Maybe something is wrong with the rooftop aerial or maybe it's the thousands of metal railings creating a Faraday cage.

'Do we have to?' he says, 'I haven't watched TV for two years. It's not good for you.'

'I just want to watch the news.'

Through the electronic snow the prime minister announces that the search for more bodies from the Christmas Island boat disaster has been called off. Under the fuzzy red dye she says, 'There is no expectation of finding any survivors or, tragically, dead bodies.'

Perhaps they will wash up in ones and twos between the rocks of the island in the next days and weeks. Perhaps they have literally been swallowed by the sea and its creatures. There will be families in Iraq who will never know, who will have a gap in their hearts that simply grows wider with the years, as wide as the Indian Ocean. I turn the television off.

His sister arrives, having come from Adelaide for Christmas like us. After dinner they head off together into the night, back towards his place.

'Don't walk through Redfern!' our friend calls after them, but they just turn their heads and laugh.

Mise en Scène

I dream the films I'll never make.
They have misty titles like
'Boy at a Window', 'Shadow of a Dog',
'Odalisque/Oblique'. They would play
short seasons in empty cinemas.
'Self Portraits' consists of fake after fake.
'Young Loves or the Fang of Time'
is shot with persistent, nostalgic lust
in black and white and blurs of poppy.
'South Coast Trilogy' has the distant haze
of over-exposure, of things long lost
that no longer matter, except to me –
flying sometimes, crawling sometimes,
from too much memory.

Stratocumulus

A rearing horse.
A Balinese
winged woman,
arms stretched forward
in spooky flight.
An exact map of Ireland
mirror-flipped, left to right.

I think the name, the officialese,
is stratocumulus.
But who cares?
Embracing the mood,
we're absent without leave
running into the windy hills.
Fine days these
for shifting shapes.

Now incoming low
is a Lancaster bomber
all in white,
a big-eared cat,
and more angels of disappearance,
which, lying here,
we know we are too –
listening to the race and rush
of the drying grass.

Long-serving Public Servants

There are not many of us left,
the old lags
doing a 40 year stretch –
lees in the federal jugs.

Our cells are personalised,
grandkids' drawings on the walls.
Lunchtime in the exercise
yard, we're left alone on our strolls.

The new breed of screw interacts
with us via email.
Short-term contracts
shift them from jail to jail.

Days seem brief and endless.
We take our patch of sun
beside the canteen glass.
The daily special is repetition.

There'll be a big card and a staff farewell
when we finally walk out of the gates.
Some young governor for his spiel
will have to call our retired mates

to ascertain
who we were.
We did our time.
The crime lay there.

Spring Café

The plane trees of Cooper St
sprinkle coffee flowers
on coffee foam.

Ready to hustle,
the boys and girls in black suits
have new haircuts,
are holding smokes and folders
and paper cups.

In the dress shops
the new season is plane-tree green
and above the knee.

Platinum madam
at the end table
does the brothel accounts.
She loves the urgency of spring.

Distracted as always,
I've forgotten to stir.

The last half of this cup
is sweet and strong
and full of flowers.

Radio News

Yawn und Drang.
The intonations of complaint,
the tinnitus of politics:
A wants what B's got,
B responds with grabs, stings and bites.
Sly dogs and poll cats.
Briefly the horror over there,
and then the sport.
Happy that we won,
gutted by the loss.
The boys did great.
The girls were on fire.
Tomorrow –
winds light to variable,
a partly cloudy day.

Skiing in Dubai

'The world's largest Snow Park is nowhere else but
at Ski Dubai. Lying on 3000 square meters of snow,
the park is a one of a kind attraction that leaves you
breathless.'

A plastic chair is somersaulting down the road,
'unprecedented' lows out east –
so let's go skiing in Dubai.

Lights at the intersection flash cold fire,
water on the tarmac blown to horizontal smoke –
so let's go skiing in Dubai.

Workers in their acid yellow coats
unthread wire from branch, branch from wire –
so let's go skiing in Dubai.

Up the coast a wood-whale groans,
lifts off its stumps and lumbers out to sea –
so let's go skiing in Dubai.

Failed crops, typhoons, the distant news comes home,
the old folks drowned on their own settee –
meanwhile, we're skiing in Dubai.

Gaudi and the Light

1.

The light is dry in Park Güell. The stone walls wear capes of bougainvillea. The hills are planted with pine, loquat, carob, and olive, with an understorey of prickly pear and oleander. Pigeons, sparrows, and a species of light-green parrot busy the air. Barcelona below stretches luxuriously to the sea. On this estate Antoni Gaudi lived for most of the last twenty years of his life, in a demonstration house for a failed real estate project. The house wasn't designed by him, though the park's entrance pavilion, terrace, viaduct, stairways and fountains were. Only two houses were built, one of which Gaudi bought himself on the advice of his patron Eusebi Güell, who lived nearby in the existing mansion of the estate.

The pious celibate Gaudi moved into the house in 1906 with his niece and elderly father. What catches my attention in Gaudi's house, which is now a museum, is his toilet seat. The usual oval shape is interrupted by two concave half circles at the front. I wonder if he wanted a shape that fitted the back of the legs better, or simply preferred a more complex curve inspired by something he saw in nature? His furniture and architectural forms resemble bones, corals, seeds, fruits, and the insides of seashells. They are made up of curves derived from straight lines: 'the straight line is the expression of the infinite' he said, thinking how a little mathematics applied to straight lines could produce the same shapes as sunflowers, grass tips, and the buds of plants that grew on his building sites. He noted parabolas in the buttressed roots of figs and kapoks and designed them into his columns and walls. He utilised spirals, honeycombs, the planoid surfaces of magnolia leaves. The four-armed crosses on top of his cathedral are drawn from the pine cones of cypresses, and the light wells resemble the shape of Protozoa.

He said, 'The great book, always open and which we should make an effort to read, is that of nature.' The catenary curve, which is produced by the force of gravity on a straight line suspended in two places, such as in a chain fence or a spider's web, he thought of as the embodiment of 'perfection' and considered it his religious 'duty' to use it in his designs.

There had always been an aestheticism within him; his reverence of nature combined with an early drive towards utopian socialism, ongoing vegetarianism and a sometimes dangerous tendency to fast. Though a famous architect, he embraced a Franciscan concept of holy poverty. His neglect of such worldly details as the condition of his clothes may even have brought about his death. On his daily walk to confession he was hit by a tram. By this time, 1926, he was in the habit of wearing threadbare suits, and he didn't carry identity papers. The tram driver described Gaudi as 'a homeless drunk who was not looking where he was going'.

Shamefully, he was left unconscious in the street. What does that say about the times and would it really be so different today? At last a policeman took him in a taxi to the pauper's hospital, Santa Creu, but it was too late to save him and he died there three days later. In the hospital, his underpants were found to be held together with safety pins.

Gaudi's style teeters on the edge of kitsch, but none the less represents a unique vision that a whole city has finally embraced and turned into a huge source of income. Each year more tourists visit the Sagrada Familia than either the Alhambra or the Prado. The souvenir shops of Barcelona are full of his imagery. It wasn't always so. For decades after his death, his work was looked down upon, seen as vaguely embarrassing. Casa Mila, one of his most important buildings, was nicknamed 'La Pedrera', 'the quarry', because the locals thought it looked like an ugly pile of rocks. Almost all his commissions came from private patrons or his connections within Catholic organisations. The city of Barcelona itself only ever gave him one job; the design of some lamp posts. He was often in conflict with the city authorities over his flamboyant breaches of their building codes.

This exotic fruity modernism, now world-famous, flowered inside the mind of an increasingly doctrinaire Catholic who said his prayers twice a day on his kneeling chair, facing the wall and the crucifix at the end of his single bed. His monkish embrace of poverty was driven by his belief that sacrifice was the true act of love, and yet his buildings are so extravagant. There was a fascinating mix of rigidity and fluidity in his character; the straight line and the curve.

His true obsession was not line, but light. He said, 'glory is light, the light of joy is the soul's pleasure' and for him, architecture was 'the transportation and ordering of the light'. In his cathedral, Gaudi wanted the congregation to feel like it was sitting in a forest of giant trees, with light pouring through the branches to an understorey of flowers.

2.

The morning I visit the Sagrada, storm clouds are approaching Barcelona. I have a back view of the town from my terrace. This is a place of chimney pots, and TV aerials behind the facades of Gracia. The aerials look like complicated fishing gear, or against the storm clouds, like intricate oriental writing, very ancient, never yet deciphered. Here is where odd things are stored, small lemon trees grown on rusty balconies. It's a place of pipes and wires and strung things, where the air conditioners breathe out. Suddenly the sun cuts under the clouds. One of them resembles for a moment Joan Miro's painting *The White Glove*, a hand floating in the sky, and I think of the freedom in that work, and how all our best art is free; as complex as that, as simple as that. Swallows spiral before the rain front.

When I enter Gaudi's cathedral I'm surprised by

how much it affects me. There are tears in my eyes as I walk, chin up, head pressed back into shoulder blades, through the glory (glory seems the right word here) of the light and space. Is it a deep memory of a religion I grew up in, but then dismissed as a dangerous cult with a bad record of child abuse? Behind all this effort, the intense labour of building a cathedral that began one hundred years ago and will take another twenty-five years to finish even with modern technology, is a glaring question. Does religion, any religion, do more harm in the world than good?

Later, on my way back home from the cathedral, I'm inexplicably drawn to open the door of a small church. Inside I see empty pews in front of a black iron grille. Behind the grille glitters the golden scrollery of religion. In these places I always feel the iron, not the gold. But then, in the empty church, I hear female voices muttering, chanting low. Are the carved saints talking Catalan to me? Is this a conversion moment? It's not until I come right up to the grille that I see them, prostrate, totally covered in white sheets like ghosts. The nuns don't know I'm here and continue their recitations and I stand there listening to them. Then I turn and leave silently, embarrassed both by my temporary alarm and my intrusion. Those living women in their white shrouds; something about it horrifies me.

I wonder if Gaudi's celibacy also had a religious basis? His niece Rosa Egea said that her uncle simply had no interest in women. In his youth he was handsome, but clumsily shy, and inclined to lose his temper quickly. A romantic myth has grown up around his one failed proposal, as though the pain of this rejection was behind all his subsequent art. There is no question that the refusal hurt him deeply when he was in his twenties, but the idea that it drove his whole life as a businessman and architect is nonsense.

The woman in question was Pepeta Moreu. Gaudi met her in 1884 at the Mataro cooperative textile mill, an early and successful example of a worker-owned factory. She was teaching French and piano there and running the kindergarten, and he was building workers' housing. He was twenty-two. They shared socialist ideals. Pepeta had already been married to Joan Palau, a soldier and trader in North Africa. He was a drinker and a gambler and violent to her, finally leaving her in Oran when she was pregnant with their child. She played piano in a café to make a living. There were rumours of prostitution, but Pepeta's biographer, Ana Maria Ferin, says this is merely slander against an adventurous, free-thinking young woman who happened to find herself in difficult circumstances.

With her parents' help she returned home to Mataro where her daughter was born, but the child died at the age of three from diphtheria. Gaudi often visited Pepeta at her parents' house, and waited until her formal divorce from Joan Palau before proposing to her. She refused him. Though they shared political viewpoints she was repulsed by his social clumsiness, and his tendency to leave food caught in his beard. Besides, another man had beaten him to it. She had already agreed to marry the builder Joseph Caballol. Gaudi was devastated and embittered. Joseph and Pepeta had four children, and a happy life together. When Caballol died, Pepeta married the wealthy businessman Joseph Vidal, and she opened her own fancy hat shop in Barcelona, becoming a successful fashion designer. For a time, Gaudi lived in the same street as her, Disputacio, and watched her come and go. Pepeta outlived him, dying in 1938 from Parkinson's disease.

By 1912, Gaudi was living alone in the Park Güell house. There is still a sense of lonely austerity here. His ninety-three-year-old father had died not long after moving in, and his niece died at the age of thirty-six. He had been her guardian since the death of his sister (also called Rosa) in 1879. Gaudi was the only one of his siblings to outlive his parents, and his niece was the only offspring. A huge shadow of mortality loomed over him. Increasingly he looked for consolation in his religion, dedicating himself entirely to its rituals and the building of the Sagrada. In the last months of his life he moved into his workshop in the basement of the cathedral itself. Of course he didn't know they were his last months, and though he was an old man, he was still hoping to live long enough to see much more of the Sagrada Familia completed.

His workshop was a gloomy space of plans, models, and sculptures in progress. In the shadows was an agonising crucifixion figure, the body a taught bow, as the nails tore through the hands. On the walls were photographs of the mosaics of Ravenna. The workshop smelt of eucalyptus. Gaudi kept a pot of eucalyptus tea boiling on top of the stove to keep away mosquitoes and alleviate his rheumatism in the damp basement.

And then there was his bed. Pushed right into the darkest corner as though he was already laid in the crypt. His eternally single bed. A check blanket. A view of nothing.

His workshop was burnt by the Anarchists during the Spanish Civil War. All his plans and drawings and models went up in smoke. I wonder if he'd lived into these times, would it have challenged his faith to see how the Catholic Church formed an unholy trinity with the royal family and the Fascists during the conflict? Somehow, I doubt it.

3.
This morning I woke up and the sun filled the eastern window and the swallows were there as always. I sliced a white nectarine and ate it slowly for breakfast, each wedge sweet as the summer light. I watched the steam from the red amber of my cup of tea drift back in the breeze from the window. It's Sunday and I think of that poem by Wallace Stevens:

Complacencies of the peignoir, and late
Coffee and oranges in a sunny chair,

And the green freedom of a cockatoo
Upon a rug mingle to dissipate
The holy hush of ancient sacrifice.

It raises the same questions for me as Gaudi's cathedral. The colours and sunny light such opposites to the dark sacrificial religion, the weird bloodiness of its torture-cross, and tombs and coldly distant god. In the Stevens poem, the woman, enjoying her secular Sunday morning, says

But in contentment I still feel
The need of some imperishable bliss.

'Yes, the temporal thing,' I might answer, putting down my cup, if I was sitting there with her. 'The feeling that all this is not adding up, just a parade of pleasant or unpleasant sensation; at best a Matisse, at worst an Otto Dix. This swallows' flight of a life.'

But the poem concludes that all we have is nature and our imagination (which is part of nature though it dreams things that are not) and both are perishable. The final lines go to the pigeons which fly 'downward to darkness on extended wings'.

Here, this morning, there are no pigeons, but the swallows, as ever, lift into the light.

Gallery

I would like to walk into
a painting by Camille Pissarro,
a foggy morning, pink and blue,
on the Seine, by the Louvre,
the trees in their winter scribble,
about 1901.

I'd buy bread and coffee
from the women in black shawls
with the scent of snow.
I'd tell them about the wars coming –
though no one would listen.

I'd try again in a Lautrec
over a *vin ordinaire*
served by the blowsy girl
with the round red face
who'll think I'm crazy
banging on about Sarajevo.
She'll pour me another
and one for herself.

I would leave then,
and not come back to the Chaïm Soutine –
far too late to try again.

Back Again

Went out a door in Prague summer,
came into this wintry house in Adelaide;
hibernation time again
on the forgetting side of the world.
Temporary, horizontal, raw ...
suburbs that seem to say
'don't get any grand ideas –
you and this sea of sheds'.

Now we lie close in the middle of the bed
remembering the warmth
our children came from.
Awake before dawn,
I listen to your lagged breathing,
imagine how cruel it would be here without you.
Would this house be a burial cave,
or would I dig myself out again?

The moonlight, even in winter,
is clearer and brighter here,
and there are birds instead of bolls.
Our magpie (we call it ours)
tries its run of notes, falters, repeats;
like our writing and art careers.

I regret switching on the radio –
a voice from the regime
boasts its 'perfect score'
turning away the desperate.
We will lose our public service jobs,
retreat to our gardens,
drink alcohol around the fire,
protest, write blogs, and wait
for the unauthorised return –
summer shining there under the door.

A Country Wedding

I'm thinking about the ground below. I can track it in my mind, all the way from South Australia to southern Queensland, the changes in the landscape from dry brown to humid green, all those petrol stations and country bakeries where we used to stop. Now a two-hour flight, it was once a three-day car journey, when the children were small and we had no money for planes. In a previous century, the same trip would have taken weeks. You wouldn't have undertaken it just for a nephew's wedding. Speed has connected, but also isolated us. The other passengers are glimpsed at loading and unloading, and remain utter strangers, though we've travelled all this way together. Yes, we could have talked, but the fact is, we didn't need to.

On the first night at the farm, as we sit around the campfire, my daughter asks me to name the stars above us. I begin by pointing out Scorpio, tracing the T-junction of its head, then moving down the long loop to the dying orange star Antares, finally curving round to the sting in the tail. She listens, then brings out her mobile phone. Holding it up to the sky, she photographs the heavens, engaging her star-map application. The phone works out our global position, and based on the exact time, superimposes a labelled map of that part of the sky, complete with information boxes about the constellations. 'Yep, pretty good,' she says. I realise how much better the phone is than my humble tour of the six or seven star groups I can name tonight, and my increasingly haphazard recall of detail, but I am so grateful for her asking.

Next morning, a still life on the veranda: nail polish, bobby pins and beers. Colour is gendered: duck-wing green, magenta, kingfisher blue, attend the bride; black suits trail across the paddock. An hour before, the groom was getting his hair cut, sitting on a chair down at the creek flat, holding a smoke and a cup of tea, like a man's last wish. Now the clans, the horses, the white cockatoos, the whole green-blue day is looking on. The lightning-struck child sings to himself in the front row of plastic chairs under the hoop pine.

Sun to seed to grass to flame, to seed again, to sun.

During the ceremony, the groom's middle name is read out, a name he shares with his dead grandfather. Suddenly I see the old man there, standing in the trees just beyond the circle of chairs. When the formalities are over, I take a walk by the creek. I'm thinking about return, the promise of completion. The creek is actually the Mary River, but its flow is much reduced now. Last year in the big floods, it tore out trees, cut new banks, bulldozed rocks and sand high up onto the plain. The she-oaks still look ravaged, as if attacked by blunt axes. But the firetail finches have returned, and the rainbow bee-eaters. There is invisible mending here all around me.

∞

I am not the only one on the planet without a mobile phone, but we are becoming rarer and more isolated. For me, it's a conscious choice to be more present, less virtual, but then I hear a good argument for getting one. It's from the DJ for the wedding, a man in his late fifties. He walks with a limp and his right shoe is one of those special built-up sorts. He used to work in the cement business. One day he was by himself at the plant and his undone bootlace wrapped round the crusher. The machine pulled his right foot in, ground away his boot, his sock, the top layer of skin. He couldn't reach the emergency stop button but he managed to get his mobile out of his pocket, hit redial and scream into it. The call went through to his boss who sped back to the site. Meanwhile the crusher kept eating; first through his ankle bone, then the flesh and other bones of his instep. He had a heart attack and lost consciousness, but the boss got him to hospital and he survived. He says he likes DJ work better than cement anyway. His music is good; we're all dancing.

∞

Now it's the finale of the wedding night. Some of the young crew are fire-twirlers, so we have a whole troupe juggling batons and spinning flaming rods in the air. Together, the bride and groom light a fire lantern. It's a Thai design, a rice-paper cage about as tall as a man. In the centre is a metal holder containing rags soaked in kerosene and lamp oil. At first the glowing lantern looks too large and cumbersome to fly. It lifts off the ground, but sways only a few metres above our heads. It seems a risky symbol to use for a marriage, but then, as if making up its mind to go all out, it rises rapidly. We imagined it might go for a few hundred metres before it burnt up and snowed back down as black ash, but this lantern really flies. It must be a thousand metres up by now. The light of a passing small aircraft seems to be on collision course. Higher, and further to the west the lantern goes, until it is another orange star in Scorpio. I watch until I can no longer distinguish it among the fine-grained constellations, but I never actually see it go out.

List of photographs

Acknowledgements

*The Adelaide Review; Australian Book Review;
Australian Love Poems 2013; Australian Poetry Journal;
Best Australian Poems 2010, 2011, 2012; Best Australian
Stories 2010; The Canberra Times; Cuttlefish; Island;
Mascara Literary Review; Meanjin; Sunday Herald; The
Turnrow Anthology of Contemporary Australian Poetry
(USA); Warwick Review (UK); Weekend Australian;
and Wet Ink.*

Warm thanks to the editors.

Wakefield Press is an independent publishing and
distribution company based in Adelaide, South Australia.
We love good stories and publish beautiful books.
To see our full range of books, please visit our website at
wakefieldpress.com.au
where all titles are available for purchase.
To keep up with our latest releases, news and events,
subscribe to our monthly newsletter.

Find us!

Facebook: facebook.com/wakefield.press
Twitter: twitter.com/wakefieldpress
Instagram: instagram.com/wakefieldpress

Printed in the USA
CPSIA information can be obtained
at www.ICGtesting.com
LVHW051005030324
773401LV00012B/1111

9 781743 054079